The Magic of Manifesting

Master the Advanced Techniques from Law of Attraction and Successfully Attract Your Desires

Todd Hoyt

© Copyright 2020 - **All rights reserved.**

The content contained within this book may not be reproduced, duplicated or transmitted without direct written permission from the author or the publisher.

Under no circumstances will any blame or legal responsibility be held against the publisher, or author, for any damages, reparation, or monetary loss due to the information contained within this book, either directly or indirectly.

Legal Notice:

This book is copyright protected. It is only for personal use. You cannot amend, distribute, sell, use, quote or paraphrase any part, or the content within this book, without the consent of the author or publisher.

Disclaimer Notice:

Please note the information contained within this document is for educational and entertainment purposes only. All effort has been executed to present accurate, up to date, reliable, complete information. No warranties of any kind are declared or implied. Readers acknowledge that the author is not engaging in the rendering of legal, financial, medical or professional advice. The content within this book has been derived from various sources. Please consult a licensed professional before attempting any techniques outlined in this book.

By reading this document, the reader agrees that under no circumstances is the author responsible for any losses, direct or indirect, that are incurred as a result of the use of information contained within this document, including, but not limited to, errors, omissions, or inaccuracies.

Table of Contents

Introduction 5

Chapter 1: The Multifaceted Reality 13

Chapter 2: Unlocking the Now 29

Chapter 3: How to Align with Your Manifestation 45

Chapter 4: Heart-Mind Synchronicity 61

Chapter 5: Getting Out of Your Own Way 77

Chapter 6: Do This Every Time You Take Action 93

Chapter 7: Energy of All Things 109

Chapter 8: What it Really Takes to Manifest Wealth and Abundance 125

Chapter 9: How to Create Your Best Life 141

Chapter 10: Becoming Fully Alive 155

Conclusion 169

References 175

Introduction

How does one live their best life? Is it by taking risks or is it by simply doing the things they've always wanted to do? Well, if that is the case, should you just give up when things become tough or distasteful for you? Such questions often lead us down paths of confusion which pose more questions than answers.

This much is simple: The universe works through a set of basic laws whose existence is undeniable. Ancient spiritual teachers, through the practice of meditation, hinted at what science has only recently discovered. That nothing in this universe is constant and that everything is vibration.

Furthermore, this vibration produces an energy field; these energy fields attract and repel other fields and vibrations, which are either similar or dissimilar to them. Thus, living the life you want is simple. Simply vibrate at the energetic frequency of what you want and you will attract it into your life.

What does that sentence really mean though? Is it really that simple? If you could just think of what you want, will it really manifest into your life? Well, not quite. While the law of attraction definitely exists, it has been misinterpreted in many ways which has led to even more frustration for those who have practiced it, or to be more accurate, those who thought they were practicing it.

Like everything else, it begins with the basics.

To master anything, you need first to establish a good foundation upon which you can build. Unfortunately, a lot of the material out there about manifestation and creation miss the mark with this regard. By skipping some fundamental information, what people end up doing is running before they can crawl. Is it any wonder then, that they fail to manifest what they truly want?

The entire process of utilizing your subconscious to manifest desires is thoroughly misunderstood, and it is precisely this misunderstanding you will gain clarity on once you read this book. A vital component of the entire process of manifestation is faith. I'm not talking about faith in a religion or anything of that sort, but faith in the process.

If you don't understand the scientific and spiritual basis for manifestation techniques, you will likely not believe in them and thus, there is no way you can manifest the life you want to live, at least with ease and alignment. Faith is what moves mountains and in this case, faith is born out of "an opening of the mind to the truth . . . a plunge into the unknown," as Alan Watts famously said.

The great thing about the advanced manifestation techniques you will learn in this book is that as you read along, you will gain a bedrock of information and knowledge within you. Once this is achieved, the miraculous power of your subconscious will be apparent to you because you've already experienced it.

That's right! You've already experienced the power of creation. It's just that you don't know it yet or haven't attuned yourself to it. Much like a baby who sees water for the first time and doesn't know what it is but drinks it anyway, you are constantly co-creating things but don't know the depth or the extent of power you're utilizing.

The laws of the universe are very simple. Thus, it is crucial for you to understand the way in which all things are connected before you proceed to use them. This is where this book can help you.

Who Am I?

It all started when I was down in the dumps myself. I read a few inspirational books and started practicing spiritual techniques because of the anxiety and depression that consumed me in my early adulthood. I needed something to be able to free me from it. Decoding the process of manifestation was certainly not my primary intention!

As I progressed further into freeing my mind from egoistic thinking, I began noticing changes in my life and how they correlated back to the way my thoughts flowed. At first, I didn't really understand what was going on but soon, I began experiencing and witnessing its effects around me. Clearly, I was doing something, but what exactly was I doing?

I decided to investigate further and as I learned, I began to become consciously aware of the universal connections all around us. The law of attraction is a very real thing; it is but a small cog in the overall machinery of how the universe works. I began understanding what I was doing and in the process, found my life's passion.

For close to a decade now, I have guided people to solve deep emotional problems in their lives and helped them realize how they can achieve their goals, no matter their current life situation. All you need to do is open your eyes and the answers will find you themselves. It really is that simple — you'll soon find out!

It is possible to attract the life of your dreams. Your past is exactly that: the past. It has gone and it will never return. Now is the moment for you to begin living your real-life and attracting all that you want for it.

Manifestation in the True Reality

Time is something that has a massive grip on all of us. We live our lives by the clock and have developed Pavlovian responses to it. The minute it strikes one in the afternoon, our stomachs rumble. The minute the clock goes past eleven at night on a weekday, we feel sleepy and so on.

Here's the thing: Time is no longer an asset, but a psychological need for the ego. It's just a construct we have created to organize ourselves better.

Somewhere along the way, we forgot this and began treating time as the endgame to everything. We get caught up in our future and our past, and end up ignoring the only real component of time: the present.

Since time is a mental construct, we do not need to build our lives around it. What we need to do is choose the reality we wish to pull into the present moment. This may sound way out in left field, but it is simply the truth about how the true reality works. Your goals, aspirations and desires do not come with time but only when you change your inner perspective do you realize the true concept of shifting your reality.

Love, prosperity, and happiness are all available now. You need to realize the true reality that we are living in order to begin attracting what you want out of life. When you acknowledge this and take action, the universe responds in kind ways and sends you opportunities to lead yourself to fulfillment and happiness.

The universe is one generous machine and it gives you what you want, all the time. You are a creator and you are meant to create consciously instead of unconsciously as you've been doing thus far. You need to start recognizing the immense power you have to shift your life in the direction you want.

My Promise

True happiness is your right and is fully available to you, I guarantee it. You don't need to live in the situation you've created for yourself by living life on autopilot all the time. The information available in this book can shift your perspective on how to propel your life to greater heights.

This universal knowledge has helped people who lost everything or haven't achieved anything, realize the power they possess to manifest their best life. This book will open the eyes of those who feel they are eternally doomed to be stuck in their life situations and help them realize that they are powerful co-creators — both of the reality they currently have and the lifestyle they desire.

It is 100% possible for you to go from unhappy and broken to living a life of security and love. In return, all I ask is for you to have an open mind and trust the power that you have. Trust the universe.

Trust that it is kind and benevolent, waiting to give you everything you want out of life. It doesn't want you to unconsciously stroll through life with no sense of purpose or direction.

Open your eyes to the miracles of the universe and watch how it rewards you with its gifts. Take control of your life by realizing your creative powers right now! After all, it is the only moment in time you have.

Chapter 1: The Multifaceted Reality

Reality is at once definite and temporary. It is both absolute and relative. Depending on one's viewpoints, reality can be hell or heaven or both at the same time. Understanding reality is the first step to knowing how you can manifest anything into your life. After all, if you cannot properly understand the state of things you live in, no amount of work will help you.

People who blindly apply spiritual techniques and methods of self-improvement are a lot like those who would use a rowboat to cross a desert. They're completely ignorant of what their environment is — how it affects them or not — and end up choosing the wrong tools.

So without further adieu, let's jump in and breakdown the reality of 'reality.'

The Nature of Reality

To truly understand what reality is, we need to deconstruct the very process of creation. After all, reality is full of things we create. For example, someone afraid of dogs will be afraid of all dogs, whether they're playful or vicious. The mental creations living in their mind creates their absolute reality. So how does creation occur in the first place?

The easiest way to understand this process is to simply look around you. What do you see? A book, a computer, a phone and so on. But what are you really seeing? Well, light of course! The things you see are visible to you because they reflect waves of light back to your eyes and thus, give themselves a form.

Seeing the Light

Sunlight in and as of itself is thought of as white light. In other words, we don't associate a color to it. However, when passed through a filter, like a prism, we clearly observe a rainbow of colors emerge.

Applying a filter is simply the process of separating what we want from infinite choices.

What I mean is, if you wish to drown your room in red light, you apply a red filter to the lightbulbs and instantly, you've got yourself a red room. Similarly, you apply filters to create any other color you'd like. In other words, what you're doing is, you're removing every color except red from your light source and creating a situation where everything is red.

Our lives play out in much the same way. We receive a stream of infinite possibilities from the universe and we filter it to create a reality for ourselves. The large majority of us do this unconsciously. Think of it as you applying a green filter to your light source and then wondering why nothing you see is red? Well, change the filter!

This stream of infinite possibilities we receive is called the quantum field. This field contains information at the atomic and subatomic level about the movement of matter. Thus, it is the record of infinite parallel realities that exist based on the filters you apply to this stream. The quantum field is a complex energy structure and as such, can only be described in a theoretical manner by current physics.

Physical reality is what we interact with on a daily basis, but there is no denying that there are things we know of but cannot explain or experience. This is the metaphysical component of reality and this is where we, understandably, experience the most debate and resistance within us.

Our minds are receptors of infinite consciousness, but are not fully equipped to handle the metaphysical realities of our existence. We are always requiring proof in the form of physical reality and end up choosing only that which we can comprehend. Thus, we end up creating whatever it is we understand possible for us, whatever we believe in.

When viewed in this light, Henry Ford's quote, "Whether you believe it or don't, you're right," opens up a whole new world of possibilities, doesn't it? The infinite stream is really just a huge tree with numerous branches, all of them interconnected with one another. The filter you apply determines which reality or branch you choose.

Balance

Another aspect of the infinite stream is balance. Our lives are filled with obstacles and walls that are thrown up by other people and the constructs of our physical world. This is simply the truth of our existence. There is no reality where obstacles do not exist. Wishing them away is merely trying to go against truth and is a futile exercise.

Obstacles are major drains of energy and by giving them undue importance, we end up prioritizing them within our lives. One of the reasons unhealthy obsessions with obstacles leads to poor results is that it puts you squarely up against another fundamental truth of life. That everything is balanced.

To realize the good, you need evil. To understand the masculine, you need the feminine. Polarity is nature's way of letting us know that balance exists and reminds us of the need to stick to the middle. Buddhism refers to this as the middle path, avoiding the extremes.

The forces that are in charge of maintaining balance usually end up being destructive because they are completely opposed to your current way of being. When you build up an excess of emotion towards a particular thing in your life, nature acts swiftly to remove that excess.

A key concept to understand here is that the negative is not repulsed by the positive. Instead, the negative excess is removed by the realization of those negative thoughts. For example, the imbalance caused by discontent with a particular situation doesn't get removed by creating content. Instead, it is removed by becoming aware of your negative thought patterns.

If you overvalue something, the exact opposite happens in order to restore you to objective reality. Thus, if you really want that job and exaggerate its importance beyond its reality, you'll end up pushing it further away from you because you're out of balance.

In order to create anything in your life, a balanced intention towards that goal is required. If you're excessively critical and harsh towards yourself, the balancing forces of the universe will give you more opportunities to stop these negative thinking patterns. But it is precisely these negative thoughts that prevent us from seeing these opportunities.

This is why it is so easy to down a negative spiral. You think of a shortcoming and remove yourself from balance by overvaluing something negative and this leads to its fulfillment. This further throws you out of balance and soon, you're in a personal hell.

The importance you give something, whether excessively positive or negative, acts as a filter and propels you down your chosen branch in the infinite reality. So what is the solution here? Well, quite simply, stop being so serious all the time. The very awareness and realization that there are infinite realities for you to choose from should reduce your belief that this current reality is the only one which you're committed to.

Stop giving the barriers in your life so much importance and recognize the reality of the situation: Obstacles have to exist to maintain the existential balance in the universe. Instead of seeking to remove them, seek to move past them by focusing on what it is you wish to birth into existence. If you pay obstacles all the importance in the world, you'll only push yourself into a reality where only obstacles exist and your life is a slave to it.

Does this mean you should become comatose to life's issues and simply not care about anything? No, this is adopting the other extreme and you'll expose yourself to the harmful effect of the forces that maintain equilibrium. Instead, you need to adopt a balanced approach which really means coming to accept things as they are.

Obstacles exist and you need to find a way past them. By focusing on the solution more than the obstacle, you consciously choose the reality where it exists and soon, the obstacle exists no more. "Choose" is the operative word here. You can either choose to be miserable by exaggerating the importance of things in your life or you can choose to view reality as it is — objectively — and remain in balance with everything.

Everything is Connected

While we do have the power of choice, choice by itself distorts our reality. We are capable of losing ourselves within our world of choices and exaggerating their importance. This puts us out of equilibrium as well since in such a reality, we fail to recognize the truth that everything is one and everything is interconnected.

The infinite stream that is the quantum field is filtered from our consciousness when we only focus on which choice we need to make. It prevents us from being overwhelmed by the realization of the full stream of consciousness. In our everyday lives, we rarely scratch the surface and realize this full stream thanks to our fixations on the choice we apply. We slip into dualistic thinking, which implies "either/or" and not 'both.' In other words, we think that if we choose positive, we reject the negative.

The truth is that despite this rejection, the negative still exists in a parallel reality and which means on an absolute scale, everything exists as one. Dualistic thinking leads to the imposition of a lot of negative filters since it creates scarcity within our minds. We pit ourselves against one another, thinking that we need to grab what we can while it lasts.

On an absolute level, oneness exists, and this cannot be quantified but only experienced. In order to describe it, it needs to be compared to something, and this implies duality. Absolute reality and pure consciousness are non-dual. Love is the ultimate expression of oneness. It implies the fusion of souls — when you love everything around you, it is impossible to cause harm, much less create negativity.

When we connect with the power of love, we no longer communicate with our minds, instead we communicate with souls. The soul is merely an expression of and a part of oneness.

The Power of the Soul

The soul has awareness of everything that is and will be. It has access to all our parallel realities and the implications of our choices. In other words, it knows which branch we're currently on, which ones we avoided, and where certain filters will take us. It knows the consequences of these choices and will warn us of negative ones.

This communication doesn't occur through our thoughts, rather it occurs through our emotions — our gut instinct, that nudge in our heart, that spidey sense we feel instinctually — which is the language of oneness. Happiness and a feeling of comfort after making a choice is an indication of your soul commending you on a choice that will benefit you. Constant discomfort and feelings of stress, negativity, and resistance are indicators that your soul has seen the consequences of this decision and does not recommend it.

Intuition or a "sixth sense" is inherent within each of us. It helps us tune into our soul while recognizing and interpreting these messages from our soul. Thus, open your mind and really listen to what your soul is telling you. Invariably, you'll find yourself along the right path. This will lead to you swimming the river of life the right way.

People usually treat the act of living with an imbalanced view. They either drift along aimlessly and go where life takes them or they swim ferociously against the current, trying to teach life a lesson — challenging the natural balance of life. Both of these ways will result in negative realities because the former removes all elements of choice and the latter simply results in removing the connection of the mind and the soul from their existence.

Accepting reality is misunderstood as simply going with the flow, but this isn't the truth. The true way to live is to simply go towards what you want, consciously, while accepting the reality of what is around you. It is expressing your intention to bring something into your life and communicating this to your soul, recognizing that all obstacles exist.

You also recognize that by traveling towards this intention, you're simply choosing a particular branch in your tree of life and since this is infinite, your intended destination exists in some form or another. Your soul knows what is best for you and is constantly communicating with you, thus your job is to simply move in the direction it points you toward, without resistance and in constant communication.

Thus, be on the lookout for signs of your soul communicating with you and be wary of complicated solutions. Often, by simply aligning yourself with the world, you'll find that the solutions to your obstacles are pretty simple and they keep you balanced instead of feeling obligated to expend great effort or make sacrifices for them.

Understanding Choice

Choices govern every aspect of our life, and there is simply no avoiding it. What you choose is up to you, and your choices are what create your reality. Your choices are what propel you along a path through your tree of life. The emotions you experience while choosing a certain outcome are what helps you birth more of these choices into your reality. It is what impacts and influences your future choices. You can choose to ignore your soul — how it is interconnected to everything — and thereby expose yourself to the equilibrium forces which will push you along a path that is hellish for you. Alternatively, you could listen to your soul and create positive emotions and changes in your life, thus maintaining balance.

Emotions transmit energy into the quantum field, hence manifesting your meta-realities into realities around you.

How to Act

It's one thing to say that you should listen to your soul and pay attention to positive emotion, but how do you actually go about doing this? Well, it all begins in the present moment by declaring your intention to create what it is you want the most in your life and taking ownership of creating that reality.

The purpose of declaring this intention is to recognize that the only one in command is you. It is simply bringing together everything that you've learned thus far into one conscious act of declaration. Whether the goal is achievable or not is beside the point. Your intention and your soul are not concerned with any of that. All that matters is that you've decided to go somewhere — create a different reality, choose a different lifestyle for yourself — and now you need to act.

As you move along your path, remember to always activate positive emotions from your soul by letting it guide you along the way. Let your choices along your path be guided by the emotions you feel and let them keep you balanced — away from the destructive forces of equilibrium. Your choices are the same as the filters you apply to the light color of your choice, as we saw previously.

Apply positive filters full of images that feel good to you, deep down. Do not adopt someone else's filters or filters which you think society will accept. This gives undue importance to your obstacles and will throw you off balance. Focus inward and prioritize yourself — your desires, your vision of the life you want to live — to determine what sort of filters make you feel good.

Some examples of filters are visual pictures and affirmations. Affirmations are positive statements that help you reinforce the idea that you are in control and you are making a conscious choice to engage with your tree of life, instead of floating around passively waiting for things to happen to you.

Visualization is a powerful tool you can use to manifest your reality. You can use visualization to manifest every single stage of your life — your desire may not arrive in the exact fashion in which you visualize them, but know that they will manifest in some form. Visualization need not only be used for what you desire in the future, but also at your current stage. Every goal can be broken down into steps and stages, and while it's great to visualize your end destination, your attention should primarily be focused on achieving what you need to achieve right now.

Thus, make this primary goal the subject of your mental images and you'll find it coming to fruition in no time. This is how you achieve your goals. Goals are based on what you consider important, and the things you consider important are the source of your joy. The thoughts and opinions of others have a right to exist, as everything does, but there's no hard and fast rule that says you need to engage with them. Stay true to your intention and proceed along your chosen path to living the life you've always wanted.

Remember, your path is yours alone; nobody else can take that journey for you. What may work for you or seem right for you can be harmful to someone else and vice versa. Always check with your soul to determine what is right for you and start acting. The only time you have is now — the present — and this is the only place where happiness exists.

By aligning your goal to your current existence, aided by the knowledge you've gained in this chapter, you'll realize true happiness in the current moment is the only place you can realize it, after all.

Chapter 2: Unlocking the Now

Happiness exists right now, but what is 'now' defined as? This poses larger and more complicated questions: What is time? Does it even exist? How real is it? All of us have had experiences where time slows down or speeds up depending on our perception of it. When working at a boring, soul-sucking job, time comes to a standstill; the clock ticks ever so slowly, each moment feels as though an eternity is passing us by.

When having a lot of fun, time literally flies. The problem is that our world is built around the concept of time and this causes a ton of conflict because time in and of itself is deluded and is against the nature of reality. This illusion will affect how we approach the idea of manifestation.

The Only Reality

Science has created wonders within our world, however we take a lot of it for granted such as the medium through which you are consuming this information: iPads, smart phones, ebook readers. None of these would have come to fruition without scientific advances. Science suffers from a peculiar condition: Despite the numerous strengths it possesses, there is one particular weakness which far outweighs all its strengths.

As a result, whenever this problem rears its head, scientific principles breakdown completely and what we're left with is simply inexplicable. This weakness is time and science's definition and treatment of it. For any real-world problem to be understood better and solved effectively, it is necessary to develop what is called a model.

A model is an idealized situation that ignores certain real-world technicalities in order to arrive at a passable solution. This approach works wonders almost always. When adapting the model solution to the real world, the solution is tweaked to account for the practicalities that were ignored and hence helping us organize our lives.

However, a huge problem occurs as this approach gains maturity. Quite simply, we forget that the model has weaknesses and start assuming that the model is an accurate reflection of reality. Scientific treatment of time has suffered from this exact problem, which has resulted in us now living in a world where things are built to an imperfect understanding of it. There is no accountability built in for non-scientific, intangible outcomes.

Model and Reality

The scientific model of time presumes it to be a straight line that always moves forward. The current moment, or the present, is simply a dot along this line. This works brilliantly as a model, but our practical experience with time shows that this is simply not true. The weaknesses of this model is proved by the fact that traditional physics breaks down when talking of quantum level phenomena, where time does not exist.

Traditional physics also breaks down when time becomes warped and Albert Einstein's musings on this confirm the fact that he clearly recognized the limitations of modeling time as a straight line. The reality is that time simply does not exist. It is a made-up construct that was created to bring order into our lives.

The current time is always 'now' and now is the only moment we have to manifest. We cannot change our past, but our lives from here on out are directly affected by what we do in this very moment to get to where we want to be. If we reject the present moment, we are rejecting reality, and rejecting reality is rejecting the possibilities of manifesting anything you desire.

Our brains work in a relative manner. This is to say that we learn better when comparing things to one another. Thus, it becomes easier to understand time by creating contrasts. That happened, this is happening, and this will happen — the past, present, and future. While contrast was originally used to bring order into our lives, we have lost sight of this. Instead, we have adopted it in a manner that causes us to be stuck, fixated, and feel chaotic at all times.

You see, time is not something that can be felt or touched. It is experienced and is thus a metaphysical reality. Time is not linear; it is constant. It never changes. It is always here and now. Science has begun realizing this and highlights the importance of the present moment in the writings of eminent physicists such as Stephen Hawking, Einstein, and David Bohm.

Dr. Bohm even went so far as to suggest that physics was wrong to assume time was a straight line; his opinions line up with much of what is taught in Zen Buddhism. One of the more insidious creations of this time as a line model is the creation of the ego. So let's take a deeper look at this.

The Ego

In order to understand the nature of manifestation it is imperative to know that time is fertile ground for the ego to grow rooted into. You see, the ego depends on this poor understanding because it needs the construct of time. Using the events of the past, it either props itself up to reject reality, or it exaggerates the importance of such events to create a hellish present. In other words, the ego can influence the direction of our lives, if we allow it to.

The ego peeks into the future and projects similar positive or negative images, all of them wildly exaggerated in order to build itself up. It is not the positivity or negativity that feeds it. Instead, it sustains itself through drama and pure emotional turmoil.

The present moment that is simply focusing on the right here/right now, lacks any drama whatsoever. This is because when you simply align yourself with presence, there is no room for drama or emotional turmoil. You simply execute what needs to be done in order to achieve your goals. It is the ego that needs to hop back and forth in time in order to build constructs.

The present moment doesn't need past and future events to propagate itself. It simply exists continuously and always, no matter what you do. Thus, when challenged in this manner, you can bet that the ego will throw all sorts of obstacles in your path which will snap you out of the present moment and plunge you into an unreal dimension of time.

Ego Dissolution

Examining the nature of the ego is the first step to overcoming it because you cannot dissolve something you don't understand. Aside from an emotional attachment to time, the ego loves judging and labeling all sorts of things. This sort of judgment usually results in the ego placing itself as inferior or superior to the object being judged. Whenever you find yourself in this frame of mind, remember that it is the ego asserting itself and you need to snap out of it. Otherwise, this will perpetuate you into a life where your ego takes control.

Another marker of the ego is its insistence on identifying with and attaching itself to objects and events. Remember that the ego loves drama. The way it uses these events is to paint itself an identity that is superior or inferior. An example of this is when the ego paints itself as the victim of unfortunate circumstances and complains about how nothing ever goes right. Victim behavior is food for the ego since by focusing on the so-called wrongdoing, it gets you to direct your energy toward it and thus, you end up having a perception of the obstacle being bigger than it actually is. You bring into play the disruptive equilibrium forces which will only intensify the strength of the obstacle, and the ego manages to prolong its control.

As you can imagine, when someone tries to come along and tell you that whatever you want is possible, thanks to the complex structure of human psychology, the ego is massively challenged. It will react in the only way it knows: by creating drama.

Focusing on the now and continuing to be incomplete presence is the best way to defeat the ego's attempts to divert you from your goals. You don't need time since time doesn't exist. It is a collection of nows. Even if you extend the field of view, every year is but a collection of todays. The present moment is the only moment that exists fully, so devote yourself to it wholeheartedly and let the ego keep making noise in the background.

The key to overcoming the ego is the same as you would any obstacle. Simply don't focus on its existence; no, this doesn't mean to pretend it doesn't exist. Instead, observe its existence with passive acceptance. Then, focus on how to get past it by focusing on the present. Do this, and you'll find the ego dissolving itself.

Psychological Time

One of the key concepts that prop up the ego is the notion of psychological time, as Eckhart Tolle calls it. In fact, he goes as far as saying that the only thing preventing us from seeing the light is time and anything that is attached to time. Thus, putting time limits on relationships or any aspect of our lives ultimately dooms it.

Psychological time is contrasted with clock time. Clock time is exactly what it means. It is a mechanical thing that we use to divide our day into manageable pieces and use to be productive. However, psychological time is a fully different beast. It is fluid and is non-linear. It jumps back and forth from the past and into the future and is never in the present. It is the ego's greatest fuel source.

Psychological time aims to transport us to the past or the future and keeps us stuck there. I mention this because it is perfectly fine to decide to finish something by say four o'clock. This is the usage of clock time. However, to travel there and always be there instead of getting the job done is to use psychological time. It almost certainly ensures we'll be unhappy.

By projecting into the future or traveling to the past, we affirm to ourselves that the present moment isn't good enough for us. In short, we're rejecting reality. By doing this, we continue to build certain structures and beliefs in our minds — which we think will comfort us and reassure us — but instead, they are merely creating obstacles on our journey to achieving our best lives.

Hence, you end up trapping yourself in your own mind and strengthening the stronghold your problems have over you. Combating the grip of psychological time can be tough since it is easy to be misled. Much like how not focusing on your obstacles can be misinterpreted to mean that you "don't care about them," not paying heed to psychological time can be construed as though you are in denial and choosing to ignore your problems.

Of course, this is not the right way to go about it. Instead, focus on the existence of solutions and give your emotions the space they need to coexist with each other comfortably. A lot of time traveling occurs because we reject the validity of our emotions, especially negative ones, instead of fully feeling each emotion. Remember that everything has a reason to exist, whether you understand it or not. Feelings of sadness and anxiety exist for a reason. Problems only occur when our emotions are imbalanced, where the negative outweighs the positive and vice versa.

If you are currently in a tough situation and if the present moment is extremely painful, allow yourself to express the negative emotions that are surfacing within you. Do not think that it is wrong to feel such emotions or that they are invalid, since doing so will cause you to travel back into the past or future to seek solace. Focus on what you can do to make the situation better, right in this moment.

If there isn't anything you can do to remedy the situation in the moment, that's okay, simply acknowledge its existence. Know that since there is nothing to be done right now, except wait for the right moment. At first, this will be quite a struggle, but over time, you'll find yourself getting better at it.

There are some techniques you can use to loosen the grip of psychological time and the ego over your life and live fully in the present moment. Remember it will be tough at first if you're used to time-traveling quite a lot. Your ego will vehemently reject these, but with persistence, you'll find yourself living more and more in the 'now.'

Technique #1: Sticky Thoughts Technique

The first practice you can implement takes advantage of the fact that your thoughts have a sticky quality to it. What I mean is that once a thought snowballs, it perpetuates itself, and once it gets rolling, it can be extremely difficult to snap out of. Those who have experience with anxious thoughts and fear know what I'm referring to. Once those thoughts start spinning rampantly in your mind, no matter what you do, it seems as if they keep pulling you back under their spell.

Well, the objective is to use this stickiness to your advantage. If your thoughts have to be sticky, why not make them positive? Why not adopt thought patterns that make you feel good and self-perpetuate on those instead? Well, this is easier said than done. The negative spiral will eventually draw you back in, even if it needs to take long detours.

One way to combat this is advance preparation. When you're feeling calm and at peace or simply not negative, take the time to visualize a mental frame of what you want to manifest. This frame should be four to ten seconds long. Fill it with all the things you want and things that bring you peace. Draw from memory or from fantasy, it doesn't matter. Through more practice, it will become more vivid and detailed. Make this frame as real as possible to pull it into the present moment.

Whenever you find your negative thoughts becoming excessively sticky, recall your happy place within your memory and use the momentum that has been built to perpetuate the positive thought. You'll find yourself feeling lighter and your mind calming down. Your level of awareness determines how early you can nip the negative thought process in the bud. The more aware you are, the quicker you can deploy your happy place thoughts and make them stick.

Technique #2: Observing the Ego

Developing your awareness is the objective of the second practice. Call it mindfulness or meditation or whatever you want, learning to simply observe and not interact with your thoughts emotionally will help you detach yourself from the ministrations of the ego. Allowing you to make the decisions necessary to guide you towards your desires. The best way to carry this out is to build up your strength.

Start by setting aside a few minutes daily to observe your breath. You'll find that your mind will wander and it is impossible to maintain focus, even for a few seconds. This is fine and is completely normal. The objective here isn't to achieve divinity or some absurd notion but to simply observe and not judge. Every time your mind wanders off, bring it back gently and focus on your breath. Think of it as a child who doesn't know what they are doing.

As you go about your day, put as much focus as possible onto what you're experiencing and thinking, without judgment. For example, if you're washing your dishes, feel the water on your fingers, the dish soap, etc. Notice what is running through your mind and do not judge or label anything.

If you find yourself in an egoistic frame of mind, then accept it and simply move on, continuing to observe what you're experiencing. Pay special heed to what your senses are communicating to you and feel them. Paying attention to what you're feeling in the moment via your senses is the best way of getting your mind to live in the present moment.

This is a powerful act, which, when done repeatedly, deactivates the ego and brings about a sense of peace and calm. As you've already learned, one of the key supporters of the ego is the notion of psychological time. The best way to undermine your reliance on psychological time is to use clock time and to stay present while you use it.

Technique #3: Using Clock Time

For example, set long term goals and visualize them when you're free. However, when the time comes to work on them, focus solely on the present. Use clock time to enforce this focus by setting work and rest periods according to your mind's needs. This builds discipline and also helps you gain mental clarity on its next action steps. Clock time has immense power in helping us become productive. A loss or lack of productivity usually results from a lack of goals or a lack of purpose. Defining a goal that is true to you will be discussed in a later chapter.

So for now, use clock time to your advantage by building a work structure that will help you achieve your goals. This is the originally intended use of time after all, so use it and see what wonders it will work for you.

Ultimately, remember that everything exists in the present moment, and no other moment exists outside of this one. Reinforce this idea into your mind and simply observe the ego doing what it does without judgment. Soon, you'll find your mind naturally focusing on the present and letting go of the need for the ego.

Chapter 3: How to Align with Your Manifestation

Change is the only constant in this universe. It just so happens that our conscious minds are singularly ill-equipped to deal with and process change. This is due to the numerous constraints placed upon it as we grow older and by the time we reach the stage of adulthood, it's almost as if our minds don't belong to us anymore.

Let's take a deeper look at this.

Social Conditioning

One of the eternal questions that surround our behaviors and beliefs is whether they're influenced and caused by nature or nurture. In other words, what is the single biggest factor that determines why we behave and act the way we do? This is exactly the subject of determinism versus free will debate.

Determinism adopts the view that our behaviors often have a root cause. Furthermore, it states these causes are always external. As such, the notion of free will is rejected since exercising free will implies that human behavior can be controlled internally. Thus, all our behaviors are predictable and can be controlled and influenced by the environment around us and the incentives it offers.

Please note that the word external here is used in the context of the mind's ability to make decisions. There are a number of behaviors that are influenced by internal physical processes such as mental health, hormones, and so on. These are always the underlying causes of human behavior, and as such, the mind is powerless to reject them and acts appropriately. Such behavior is said to be influenced by internal determinism.

External determinism is when your behaviors are influenced by factors outside your physical body. It must be noted that determinism is but a model and should not be taken as a gospel truth. Indeed, the fact that psychologists cannot accurately predict a person's behavior has led to two levels of determinism forming, called hard and soft.

Hard determinism refers to those points of view where humans are viewed as nothing but biological machines and seek to impose rationality over behavior. Soft determinism is where instead of treating people as machines, some fraction of free-will is recognized. Conditions are viewed as 'likely' causing certain behaviors instead of outright saying they 'definitely' cause them.

Determinism also runs up against common social mores such as responsibility and morality. For example, if someone is on trial for murder and isn't insane and hasn't done it out of self-defense or unconsciously, it is pretty hard to justify the hard determinist approach of saying that this person had no choice in the matter.

Free will theory is an approach that is completely against the Determinism and its approach toward human behavior. Free will rejects the notion that all behavior can be predicted and that humans have no choice in determining their reactions to triggers. Free will is, in fact, seen as an important difference between human beings and other animals in our world.

Choice

Our ability to exercise our free will is what allows us to have control over our destiny. No other living being on the planet has this capability. In fact, the degree to which a species rejects deterministic triggers is an indicator of their average intelligence. This effect can be seen in human beings as well. Those considered free thinkers and major influencers of human society are often seen as being apart from the masses, accepting widely held beliefs.

Beliefs thus are formed thanks to deterministic forces during our upbringing and we unquestioningly adopt them. However, as our consciousness grows, so does our ability to select and adopt beliefs that help us grow. Yet, we remain slaves to our old beliefs and our needs to follow the deterministic way of living.

The key for you to realize is that you are subject to both forces — determinism and free will. One seeks to place you under the control of a mass mind and adopt its beliefs, whether they are right for you or not. The other, free will, is your expression of who you truly are. It comes not from a place of fear or resistance, but via communication from the soul itself.

In order to break your shackles and rid yourself of the diseases of the mass mind, you need to recognize your ability to exercise your will and quite simply, your right to do so. Far too many of us go around wearing the right masks and saying the right things to just fit in.

Instead, you need to connect with who you truly are and using your free will, express yourself fully as nature intended you to.

Emotional Adaptation

When you exercise your choice to recognize true reality and express yourself as nature intended you to, you'll find that your mind doesn't quite follow your lead willingly at first. Instead, it will remain stuck in its old patterns for a while and seek to placate the ego by time traveling.

As it travels and as you begin redirecting it patiently back to the present, you'll find that the negative emotions which the ego seeks to create by time travelling will be brought into the present moment. This is a particularly problematic thing because our first instinct is to run away from the negative instead of letting it surface and tune into the learning lessons it is trying to offer us.

We often face negativity by covering it up with something else or substituting it with positive emotion. The thing to do instead is to simply allow it to exist and not give it energy by prioritizing it. Let it simply exist. It has a right to exist, so acknowledge that by doing so, you're bringing into play an extremely powerful human ability: adaptability.

Adapting to our circumstances is an ingrained quality in every single one of us. It is what has enabled us to survive for this long. Adaptation helps us figure out the best way out of a negative situation and adjust to it in a manner that helps us overcome it. Resisting negative emotion, thus, only delays the adaptation process and will only make things worse.

Feelings of anxiety and depression are not combated by running away from them but by allowing them to bloom in you when they arise and letting yourself deal with it. By letting these feelings exist and receiving them, you are recruiting forces far greater than your rational mind can comprehend.

Resistance to your emotions is a lot like fighting fire with fire, and this only makes things worse. It is crucial that you do not pass any judgment on the negativity that crops up. Recognize that it exists and return to the present moment, as best as you can.

When you first start doing this, your mind will resist vehemently, but with continuous practice, it will get used to it and soon, you'll find yourself observing negative emotion passing you by like a temporary rainstorm. You'll have adapted to the situation and will no longer fear the onset of anxiety, no matter how bad your condition.

So, open yourself up and allow yourself to receive whatever emotion crops up within you.

Allowing Yourself to Have

Our existence in this world is dependant on energy flow. Energy cuts to the very essence of who we are. When describing ourselves, we may state our name, our occupation, what we do in our lives, but does any of this truly describe "I"? The truth is that there is no "I' and that we are simply a subset of energy that flows around all of creation.

There are different types of energy that work together to maintain balance and keep our existence in equilibrium. These are active energy, receptive energy, and balanced energy. The first two can be thought of as the yin and the yang of our existence while the third is simply balancing the two counter energies.

Active energy is what is valued and highly desired in our current culture. We seek people who put themselves out there and attack things with gusto. Such people are often described as 'go-getters' and so on. All of these energies have a positive and a negative side to them. While the positive side of active energy results in success and achievement, when it turns negative, it can result in aggression and a lack of restraint.

Receptive energy manifests itself as having an open mind and the willingness to adopt different points of view. This energy is more soothing in nature and often manifests itself as waiting for the right moment to act and being alert, in a state of readiness.

The achievement of a balance between these energies results in an ability to adapt to any environment and the willingness to change. When imbalanced, it often results in rigid thinking and a general fundamentalist view towards a particular viewpoint, which is really just the adoption of a particular energy.

Receptivity

Of all the three, the receptive energy is the most important since this is what determines the health of the other two types of energy. A major reason for this is that receptivity is what determines our level of acceptance. Without accepting things as they are, there can be no steps taken to either change or adapt to situations, which leads to rigidity.

When fully functional, receptive energy manifests as groundedness, awareness, and acceptance. It puts us fully in touch with who we are and the realities of our situation. With the help of active energy, we can take steps to rectify it if need be. Without the input of receptive energy, active energy becomes default, and this leads to imbalanced states where we simply won't know when to stop, so to speak.

However, the real power behind receptive energy is that it is crucial in determining our ability to give and receive love. Love is what ultimately moves the world and is the emotion that connects us directly to our soul and the infinite knowledge, as we've seen in the previous chapter.

Awareness is crucial for love to exist since love demands an attitude of leaving oneself behind and putting something else ahead of us, in a non-conditional way. Awareness is but an expression of receptive energy, as is acceptance. Both are crucial if we are to maintain the highest levels of honesty with ourselves.

Thus, to fully experience the fruits of joy, you need to allow yourself to receive. You need to open yourself to what is around you and become vulnerable to it. This doesn't mean you become a slave to it but merely open yourself up to it and know that whatever happens, you're finding your way back to your soul and that love will show you the way.

Unconditional Love

When we're born, the large majority of us receive unconditional love. Babies of any life form elicit all forms of unconditional love and happiness in all of us, and this speaks to a fundamental human need: the need to receive unconditional love. Unfortunately, the memories we have as babies fade out and we grow up not knowing what unconditional love is.

The sad truth is that there are a lot of people who have no idea of what this is and the level of imbalance it causes in our lives. We end up thinking that love is a conditional thing, to only be given when we receive something else. Conditional love is simply an example of a societal construct that gets imposed on us as we move through the world. Like most societal constructs, it is merely an illusion and is far removed from the truth.

How does one begin shedding these constructs surrounding love? Well, the first step is recognizing that unconditional love exists and is something that you fully deserve. Next, in order to receive unconditional love, you need to start giving it.

Technique #4: Becoming present with your emotions

Whatever it is that you put out into the world, is exactly what you will receive. If you choose the branch that leads to more love in your tree of life, then that is what will manifest in your physical reality. Thus, in order to receive something, you first need to give.

Now unconditional love doesn't mean you need to start confessing your love to random people around you. Far from it. Instead, understand that love is an energy form, and you need to engage with everything around you without judgment and with compassion. This is, after all, what love truly is. We're familiar, to varying degrees, on how we can express love, but how does one exude love as energy?

Well, this is simply conveying an energy of acceptance towards a particular subject. Is your coworker bothering you incessantly? Well, close your eyes and accept them for who they are and wish them the best in their lives. Wish for them to achieve everything that they want and that they receive unconditional happiness. You'll often find that by doing so, the quality of your life improves dramatically. Perhaps they no longer seem to irritate you (even if those qualities and habits still exist within them), because you have learned to accept them for who they are, flaws and all.

Release all expectations you have and simply give. Constraining your expression of love is simply trying to achieve a purpose that counteracts what you're trying to do. This really doesn't need any explanation. Initially, this might feel wrong if you're accustomed to this, but with regular practice every day, it'll become second nature to you.

Start small by practicing during the more mundane moments of your day and build your way up toward more annoying moments. Soon, you'll find yourself in a blissful world, and the best part is that this is all your own creation!

Emotions are your key to happiness, even the negative ones. Remember that every emotion exists for a reason and indicates an imbalance or function as a warning sign. Thus, you need to give your emotions the space to play out and express themselves, instead of denying them and seeking to compensate in some other manner.

Awareness via meditation or mindfulness will help you accept your emotions. Remember that they are the connection to your soul and that your soul knows what is good for you since it has access to infinite information. Thus, any action you choose to pursue seeks confirmation from your soul prior to moving forward. Mindfulness will give you the markers you need to determine this.

Technique #5: Receptivity

Open yourself up to the world and become more receptive to the energy that surrounds you. We're surrounded by miracles, but we often fail to take any note of them. Think of all the things around you right now. There's probably electricity, the internet, a computer, a smartphone. Consider how fantastic all of this would have been to someone who was born in the previous century. A lot of these miracles would have seemed like Star Trek to you when you were a kid!

Take the time to observe them. Pick one each day and truly observe it. Marvel at how ingenious its design is, even if it doesn't work properly. Consider how miraculous it is, that even a flawed computer is a miracle, requiring so many different components to be engineered precisely in order to form something. The words on your screen, the color of the things you create are all stored as energy on a disk which is then transmitted using another form of energy. As I said, we're surrounded by miracles!

Practicing minimalism is a great way to stop and recognize the miracle that is present in every individual thing. The fewer things that compete for your attention, the more time and energy you will devote to it, and the more you will appreciate it. If there was just one item in front of you, you're more likely to engage with it in a deeper, more meaningful way.

Increasing your level of receptivity has an added benefit in that you'll learn to ask better questions. Be engaging with the world in a more compassionate way; your questions will naturally end up being more open-ended. This will cause you to question a lot of your own assumptions and that of society too.

Technique #6: Detaching from Conditioning

In order to detach from our conditioning it is important for us to recognize that the stereotypical model that we live by is untrue. The roles we play in our everyday lives are a matter of convention, they are abstract. Thus our conditioned character is tangible. Learning to be mindful and observing the conditions "pop up" within our everyday thoughts, emotions, and actions is a sure way to start the process of change.

Never hesitate to ask questions when confronted with a set of norms that you are forced to follow. Focus on questions that are open-ended and elicit a wide variety of responses. Questions that force you to consider all alternate viewpoints are a great example of this. One of the best ways to reinforce the oneness of everything in this world is to simply sit down and have a discussion with someone who has the diametrically opposite viewpoint as yours.

Chapter 4: Heart-Mind Synchronicity

Your body has two major nerve centers. While one of these centers receives a lot of attention, the brain, the other, which is your heart, tends to get ignored in favor of rationality and other modern constructs. Ancient mystics have written that our minds are not just our brains but really, are a combination of our brain and heart.

The mind to brain connection is something that you need to pay attention to and nurture in order to live your best life. Let's look at how to do this but first off, let's look at what the connection even is.

The Connection

The heart has always been considered in scientific circles to be nothing more than a muscle. It is the size of your fist and pumps out blood non-stop, day by day, and when it stops, you die. Simple, really. You're advised to exercise it by performing exercises that help the cardiovascular system and eating healthy. That's all there is to it, according to science anyway.

However, recent research shows that those ancient monks were onto something. You see, the heart is much more than a blood-pumping machine. It is one of your centers of communication. As much as your brain controls your ability to communicate and make decisions, your heart controls this, to a greater extent.

In fact, your heart creates an electromagnetic field that is sixty times greater than the one your brain creates. The heart is actually an advanced processing center and has functions that enable it to remember, make decisions, and learn. The electromagnetic field that the heart produces can be detected up to several feet away from a person's body.

Even more significant is that this electromagnetic field can be used to communicate between people. When two people are in close proximity or are in physical contact with one another, communication occurs. Now, this communication is of a very different nature from the type that occurs between brains.

While the brain uses words to encode its thoughts, the primary communication device for the heart is emotion and intuition. Communication occurs between individuals who are in different emotional states. Thus, a person who is in a negative state of mind and emotion can be influenced by someone who is in a positive state or communicating love to the former.

To conclude, a person's behavior and thought patterns could absolutely be changed by the regular encouragement of positive emotions. Thus, stressful thought patterns and behaviors can be replaced over time by consciously choosing to foster positive emotions, which originate from the heart.

The keyword here is emotion. Positive thoughts don't carry a lot of weight without the emotional heft to back them up. The heart plays an important role in communicating positive emotions to the brain as it formulates thoughts. Emotions can, of course, be transferred as well from what we've seen. A lot of people have practical experience with this. Hang around someone who is extremely negative, and you will feel worse about yourself. Hang around someone positive and optimistic, and you will soon feel that nothing is out of your reach, you can achieve everything.

Studies conducted with a mother holding her baby indicate that often, the mother's brain waves synchronize with her baby's heartbeat which makes her far more sensitive to her baby's needs.

Thus, synchronizing your heart and mind is crucial for a happy existence. Modern culture has marginalized and excluded the human heart from a holistic conversation in favor of rationality and pragmatism. However, all this has done is weaken your ability to deal with the world. In fact, a vast majority of communication is nonverbal (think body language and facial expressions), and by marginalizing your heart, you're depriving yourself of a powerful means of communicating with the world.

Let go of your brain's need for rationality and judgment of anything that seems irrational or doesn't make sense traditionally. The brain loves constructing abstract models and pondering over things. The heart by contrast simply accepts without judgment. It doesn't complicate things and communicates a lot faster than the brain does.

Nurture it, and you will notice that your life improves dramatically.

The Heart Speaks

While your brain has the ability to perform gymnastics, convince you to avoid certain situations, and justify your actions — whether they're right or wrong — your heart has no such ability. Instead, the heart only knows truth and love — that is its superpower. Whenever it speaks, it only knows to speak the truth, and it does so out of a deep love for you.

The truth can sometimes hurt, especially if one is lost. This causes a lot of us to simply turn a deaf ear to the voice of our hearts. You must understand that one of the reasons we don't like hearing things that are unpleasant to us is due to judgment. Our brain specializes in judgment and when we hear negative things about ourselves, what we are really comprehending is that we are less than, we are not enough — good enough, successful enough, ambitious enough, and so on — we believe the judgment being passed onto us.

The heart has no business judging things. It accepts everything the way it is and only seeks to improve things out of deep love. The heart doesn't need or want anything; it is happy only when you are living your best life and fulfilling your purpose. The heart also knows things that you're not aware of.

You see, the heart is simply the body's connection to the soul and as such, is its primary communication device. Remember that the soul has access to infinite knowledge which is communicated to the heart. Your heart realizes that everything around you is simply a manifestation of the things you deeply believe in.

Thus, the conditions around you are not someone else's fault, but indicators of things within you that need to be addressed. It will always communicate this truth to you, but whether you choose to listen or not is up to you. A lot of people don't. They rationalize away their feelings and resist them, thereby hindering their ability to adapt and evolve, as we saw in the previous chapter.

Some of you might think that I'm advocating that one must only listen to their hearts and ignore their brain, but this is not the case. Instead, you need to take your brain and heart side by side and listen to both of them. The heart can be impetuous at times and needs the brain's help to slow it down. The brain, on the other hand, lacks the ability to decide quickly and doesn't have access to full knowledge. This is where the heart excels.

Always listen to the voice of your heart, even if you don't like what is being said. Never be afraid to open your heart to someone else for fear of being hurt. Remember that an open heart is far more powerful than anything else in this world. If you feel hurt or some negative emotion, this is simply a reminder to love yourself more and to stop running away from things, confront them instead and start taking ownership for all your emotions — they all have something to teach you.

Your heart speaks in whispers. These whispers speak and manifest as inexplicable feelings and intuition. This communication is beyond logic and reason since these are constructs of the brain. It will not make sense, and that is precisely the point. Sometimes, people struggle to differentiate between intuition and fear. The way to separate them will seem complicated at first.

Fear usually manifests itself as a physical response such as sweaty palms, racing heartbeat, etc. The only response that fear generates, when you retreat, is a relief. Intuition, on the other hand, will result in you feeling comfortable, whether you fully know what is going on or not.

So really, the key is to get familiar with the differences between the feelings of relief versus comfort. At first, these will seem the same but relief is felt to a far higher degree than comfort is. It is almost always in reaction to some negative experience, as opposed to comfort, which is felt as being at peace with things.

The key is to open up and listen to your heart. Be aware of your feelings and reactions. Also, recognize that your heart cannot speak to you when you're using your brain in a deep manner. If you attempt to access your intuition in such times, you'll end up activating your ego instead and end up being dictated by its norms and needs, which is exactly the thing to avoid.

Choosing Your Goal

When you start listening to your heart, questions about your purpose and goals become a lot clearer. Our lives are profoundly impacted by this single most pivotal question (even if we choose to ignore it): What is our true purpose in this world? Think about it for a moment; why do you get out of bed in the morning? What is your reason? What is your 'why?'

Studies conducted on lifespans reveal that the places on earth where people tend to live the longest all have one thing in common: a blue zone. Every such place has a philosophy much like the Japanese goal-setting system of Ikigai. Okinawa in Japan happens to be one of these blue zones, and this is where the concept of Ikigai originates from.

Ikigai helps clarify your life's purpose. While there haven't been any studies proving that this particularly contributes to a longer and happier life, there have been numerous studies proving that a loss of purpose does lead to shorter life spans. Your personal Ikigai lies at the intersection of these four elements.

The first element is what you love doing or your passion. The second is whether the world needs this or not. The third is whether you're good at it vocationally and finally, whether you can get paid for it and thereby make a living doing it. As you can see, these are not easy questions to answer, and at first glance, a lot of us will not have these four elements intersect with one another.

We'll explore goal setting the Ikigai way in detail in the next section, but the key to figuring it out is to listen to your heart. It has a way of pushing your thoughts in a particular direction and getting you curious about things. Follow its lead and indulge your curiosity. You never know where they will lead you.

A classic example of this is when Steve Jobs decided to attend a calligraphy class in college, purely out of curiosity. Later, the lessons he learned in this class were applied to the font on Apple's computers, and this soon became one of the major selling points for their products.

Curiosity and our sense of wonder are just a couple of things we lose as we grow older and become indoctrinated with societal conditioning.

Indulge your inner child and always be curious. Never stop exploring or take the world for granted.

Technique #7: Listening to your Intuition

The first practice which will enhance your brain and heart connection is to simply listen to your intuition. This is something which is difficult to describe since intuition is a metaphysical experience and is better felt than explained. A way of increasing your ability to be intuitive is to practice meditation or mindfulness.

Mindfulness helps you focus on the present moment and thereby eliminates distractions that cloud your judgment. Paying attention to your gut, literally, is a good way of enhancing your ability to be intuitive. Your gut is one of the places that reacts to intuitive impulses and biologically speaking, your gut health is an important marker of your overall health. As such, it is a major energy point in the body, so pay close attention to it.

Make every effort to listen to your dreams and record them as soon as you wake up. Memories of our dreams fade soon after waking, so it is crucial you do this as close to waking up as possible.

Dreams are just a manifestation of our brains processing information throughout the day. A good way to make your dreams work for you is to consciously think about the possibility of success and abundance before going to sleep. As you sleep, your subconscious mind, which has an open connection to your heart, will go to work, and upon waking up, you'll find yourself with new insight.

When your intuition strikes, make sure you listen to it. Remember, in order to listen to your heart, you need to actually open yourself up to it. If you receive a message, don't simply ignore it or dismiss it. This will simply result in you becoming deaf to your intuition and missing any messages it's trying to send you. How do you know when your heart is speaking to you?

Well, your feelings are your best guide. If a decision you've taken doesn't make logical sense, but you feel happy or light in your heart or gut, then your heart is communicating to you that this was the right course of action, even if your brain hasn't quite understood this as of yet. Increasingly lucid dreams are another indicator of your heart talking to you.

Sometimes, events in your life will set themselves up in strange ways. For example, you will find that a particular series of events constantly occur, pushing you to take a particular course of action. This is your heart asking you to do something, and the more the pattern occurs, the more you've been ignoring it. Your thoughts will also wander over to a particular pattern repeatedly.

Your heart is in constant communication with your brain, and if you don't understand what you're feeling, it then uses your brain to influence your thoughts and push you toward a particular direction. If you find this happening to you, take the time to investigate and understand what is being communicated.

If you keep ignoring the signs, eventually you might even fall sick. Ignoring what your heart is telling you and ignoring your emotions will only add stress to your life and you will succumb to it. Other physical signs include creeping anxiety or nervousness. This sickness is simply your heart communicating with you in an extreme manner so you can awaken and do what it truly wants you to do.

Technique #8: Goal-setting with Ikigai

Once you begin relying on your intuition to a greater degree, you'll find that setting your goals becomes a lot easier. The Ikigai process can become complicated by worrying too much about what the world needs. Instead, simply focus on what moves you and worry about the world later. What is it that you're curious about? Focus on this instead and move toward it.

A helpful tip to find your Ikigai is to stay active and engage your brain. This could be done by simply learning new things as much as possible. The brain loves to exercise and is capable of learning, understanding, and storing so much more than we give it credit for. Doing so will keep your mind fresh and alert while also strengthening the heart and mind connection. Stop trying to hurry things and really take the time to be present when completing any task.

Being present and grounded in your task will not only enable you to complete your work to a higher quality but will also keep you open to receiving intuitive flashes. Adopting a slow and steady pace of work is frowned upon by our societies where everything needs to be accomplished at a hurried pace and delivered "right now." This alone should convince you that adopting the opposite of this is the right way of doing things.

Ensure a good quality of life for yourself and be kind to yourself. A lot of people seem to think that goals require sacrifice and that struggle is necessary. This is simply adopting the attitude of fighting against the current, as we saw in the first chapter. You gain nothing by this and will only exhaust yourself. You've chosen to walk along a particular path, so embrace it fully and take in everything that it has to offer.

Surround yourself with people whose company you enjoy and connect with nature. Adopt simpler means of living and practice minimalism. Keep yourself active and physically fit, and be present in everything that you do. These nuggets of wisdom might not make sense from a goal-setting perspective but really, what you're doing here is simply reconnecting with the way life ought to be lived — in harmony with oneself — body, soul, and mind.

By living in a way that feels authentic to your body, mind, and heart, you are opening the connection your heart has to infinite knowledge, and you'll receive what you need to know when the time is right. Remember that finding your Ikigai is an emotional process and there isn't a step by step rational plan to follow here. You need to feel your way to it, and once you receive it, then comes the time to implement those insights and nudges from your heart by structuring it into rational plans using your brain.

Chapter 5: Getting Out of Your Own Way

The biggest obstacle to your success and happiness usually stares right back at you when you look into a mirror. We already know that by giving obstacles our attention, we only end up strengthening them. By giving our worst qualities our attention, we end up fortifying ourselves against what we really want, unintentionally.

Detachment and allowing nature to flow are crucial concepts you need to learn, and in this chapter, we're going to dive into these important concepts.

Detachment and Observing

You've made your choices and are moving along with positive emotion. You're waiting for the thing you want to manifest, but really, nothing happens. Life carries on as usual and you keep waiting. Soon, you get sick of waiting and then begin feeling anxious, which is followed by anger at your helplessness. All in all, within a short time of making your choice, you're ready to call it quits and try something else.

Sadly, this is the experience a vast majority of people go through when they choose to assume control of their lives. The prospect of assuming control, when improperly understood, leads one to believe that you can perfectly coordinate everything about your life. Well, this is true and untrue. While you can manifest every single thing you want into your life, the key to successfully manifesting things in the manner you want and everything working out exactly how you envision it is by aligning yourself with the larger reality.

Larger reality involves understanding that all things are one. It is about learning how you can and need to remain in balance and about how your parallel realities coexist. Most of all, you need to understand that you cannot always control everything, in the traditional sense. Control is something that is defined by the ego and is governed by it. When I say you need to seize control of your life back from your ego, I'm not talking about initiating a power struggle and then seeking to impose yourself on nature.

This would be much like your arm deciding to declare independence from your body and then trying to punch you. No one will be happy with that chain of events. Controlling your life is really all about giving into nature and trusting in higher intelligence. It is about trusting your heart and its connection to infinite intelligence — having faith that it knows what is good for you and will always look out for you. The idea of imposition as control is an ego-driven construct and is completely wrong.

The very idea that you can control natural processes itself reeks of self-importance, and this is a hallmark of the ego. Once you make your choice and then apply this flawed understanding to it, what you're really doing is letting your ego convince you to hand over control via a clever argument.

While the ego is in control, all that will really happen is a drama-filled existence, and you'll get this in spades since you'll be convinced that you have no 'control' whatsoever. The key to snap out of this vicious circle is understanding what control means and then practicing it through detachment.

Detachment is a state of mind where you make your choice and then stop infusing it with negative energy by worrying about it coming true. You sit back and trust the universe to give you whatever it wants. Detachment takes you out of the cycle of giving your obstacles energy, which everyone does inadvertently. By genuinely not caring about outcomes and whether or not your wish will manifest, you encourage it to appear in your life.

This seems contradictory advice. After all, by making a choice you're displaying that you care about something. So are you supposed to care or not care? Well, you certainly should care about which direction you wish to take your life in. What you should not care about is whether or not this actually happens. By caring about the outcome, what you end up doing is resisting what life gives you back.

The truth is that when we make a choice, we don't fully know what is good for us. It could be that by aiming for one choice and being fixated on it, what is really happening on a grand scale is that we're opting for something much better than the actual choice presented to us at a surface level. Think back to the example of Steve Jobs and the calligraphy class. If he stubbornly insisted on becoming an ace calligrapher, the world would have been deprived of so much wonder, and Apple — it's technology, brand, devices — as we know it would not have existed.

We don't know the repercussions of our choices; only our hearts know this. Hence it is ideal to remain open to its suggestions at all times and look out for the many signs and ways it communicates with you. By doing so, you melt away any resistance. After all, if you're actively listening to your heart and are fully present, where is the space for any resistance to exist?

Leave your fate up to nature and detach yourself from the outcomes of what you think you need the most. Be comfortable with the knowledge that whatever happens, you're being looked after and that you'll be just fine, no matter what comes your way. What will end up happening is that you will expose yourself to working and thinking in a flow state, which is really just the universe's way of guiding you to your ultimate destination.

The Open Window

What if you could live in a place where time doesn't exist and the present is the only real thing?

In this place, there is no such thing as effort, merely execution. Everything that you do is effortless and always results in a level of performance that you find awe-inspiring. Well, that place most certainly exists, and it is called the flow state, or as I like to think of it, the open window into the quantum field.

The quantum field contains all the information that exists, be it past, present, or future. It is the ultimate record of everything that has happened and all that has yet to take place. Your heart and soul have a direct connection to this information and channel this to you when you open your connection to them and are receptive. However, the large majority of us are simply not equipped within our environment to remain in a state of mind and heart that nurture this connection.

Instead, we're consumed by our daily woes and obstacles. We're fretting about this or that thing which ultimately is of no consequence, but at the moment seems like a big deal. This kind of worry is sometimes mistaken as being present, but that is certainly not the case. The very concept of worry is created by the ego since worry implies fear of something bad happening and some future state being worse than where we are right now.

This creation of contrast between the future and the present is just another way of believing in time and imposing its restrictions upon ourselves. True presence is being in the flow state and staring directly into the unlimited quantum field. This, contrary to what you might think, is not an overwhelming experience but actually the highest state of peace you can achieve.

The flow state is all about executing perfectly, and when we're carrying out an endeavor, we often stumble into this. It is the highest state of creation we can access. You often hear of athletes or musicians talking about how they don't know where the stuff they created came from, that it simply materialized in their heads. Well, this is the flow state.

Such states can occur individually or in groups. In groups, it occurs when there is a collective investment towards a goal, and everyone is fully focused on what is happening right now, in that moment. Think of an entire stadium watching and experiencing a close game in any sport. That particular moment is not something that is special individually, but if you recall, you almost always develop some sort of a connection with those who experienced it with you. This is merely the result of everyone involved being immersed into the flow state at once, as a group.

The flow state is also characterized by complete silence. As in, inner silence. The annoying voice inside your head that questions and debates your decision and causes anxiety vanishes, and you begin to fully invest in the present moment . The ultimate aim of a lot of practice, such as mindfulness or meditation, is to simply achieve this flow state.

Flow state occurs when your subconscious has been trained to such an extent that the action you wish to carry out is automatic. Your conscious brain simply shuts off and you're free to let your subconscious mind take over. Thus, the crazy thing about the flow state is that you do more by simply using less of your brain. If there was ever an explanation of how you are your own worst enemy, this is it. I mean to say that the best way to get things done and achieve peace is actually to shut down a part of your own brain.

This state is named as such because there are no obstacles in your path. You simply flow right over them as water would over rocks. You automatically know which path to take and do so without question or hesitation.

The Path of Least Resistance

If you observe anything in nature, such as a river or any living creature, you'll see how everything takes the path of least resistance. A river doesn't insist on cutting a straight line across a valley at all costs. It simply goes wherever there are lesser obstacles and maneuvers itself around the problematic areas in front of it. It doesn't stop to fight an obstacle or engage in a battle of egos.

Egos are something that are reserved for the human realm. These are erect barriers of our own making and they prevent us from taking the path of least resistance. This path is simply the shortest way to our goal, and almost always, we can't see it for what it is. We instead see it as a series of digressions and distractions, much like when we see a river snaking its way through and wonder how much faster it would be if it just took a straight line.

The path of least resistance unveils itself when we switch off our conscious mind, which contains the ego, and rely entirely on the subconscious mind which is always on but has its voice drowned out by the conscious critic. The subconscious mind is simply your true mind —the sum of your beliefs learned from consciousness and your heart's communication with the infinite. It contains everything you need to know and has a way, via the heart, to supply you with information with regards to things that you don't know yet.

The key to switching into subconscious mode is to stay present and to fully experience the present moment, without judgment, listening with an open mind and heart. Although this sounds simple enough, it is an extremely difficult thing to practice in reality, as all of us can attest. The subconscious will speak to you in many ways. Most of the time, it doesn't communicate via language, but through emotion, just like the heart.

Intuition, emotion, and feelings are how you will be given information and when you are immersed in the flow state, you'll simply know what to do. The key is to get yourself acquainted with your subconscious mind and the way to do this is by monitoring your emotional states. Understand that whenever you are under stress or are caught in a negative cycle, there is some element of time involved and that the ego is breaking your connection with the subconscious.

One of the best ways to short circuit the ego is by reducing your own importance. This is not to say that you should treat yourself poorly. Instead, notice how you are a part of the world, of nature, and not somehow above it or below it. Notice how nature nurtures everything within it and how you are a part of this circle. People who tend to struggle in their lives with unhappiness suffer from problems of the ego.

They refuse to see how, by prioritizing their ego's needs, they actually strengthen their obstacles and set a course headed right for those hurdles. Think of it like this. When walking, largely speaking, you'll go wherever you look. In the metaphysical realm, looking is done by allocating energy. Thus, whatever it is you're focusing the most energy on, that's what you're looking at and that's what you'll crash into.

Instead, finding the path of least resistance is simply looking where you're told to look. This is the exact opposite scenario of what the ego wants since the ego has to believe it is superior to everything around it. The thing guiding you on your path is your heart and your subconscious mind. Thus, by monitoring your feelings, listening to your intuition, and respecting your hunches, you figure out which path you need to take.

The flow state always directs you to the simplest solution for every problem, and the path of least resistance always lies in this direction. The flow state knows which solution to pick in advance, so don't worry about any temporary obstacles that you can foresee. If you start worrying about these, you end up engaging the ego and sure enough, your ego will lead you right into it, in direct opposition to the path of least resistance.

Instead, practice detachment. Make your choice and then relax and know that forces greater than you or I can comprehend are in motion. You're being taken toward your destination, whether you know it or not. Thus, become an observer instead of being a passenger to your ego. Trust that the universe is taking care of everything and that you will also be taken care of.

Technique #9: Detaching & Observing

Detachment is the first step to tapping into your subconscious mind and activating the flow state. Meditation remains the best way of practicing detachment, especially those practices which are dedicated to practicing equanimity, as opposed to focus. Take the time to observe your breath, without judgment, and whenever your mind wanders, simply bring it back to focus on your breath. This technique has been described before.

Take it a step further by observing the sensations occurring throughout your body and then practice observing them. Don't try to fix the condition or change it in any manner, simply observe. For example, you might be experiencing pain or numbness in your feet; your back might be stiff from sitting unsupported. Simply observe and note the sensation.

Notice how your conscious mind will react as if you're on fire and your existence is being threatened. This is simply the ego realizing it is under threat and being reactive, causing all sorts of drama. You will soon notice that the sensations ebb and flow and are not constant. Once you move past this stage, your ego will finally trick you into thinking that you're feeling tired and you'll be lured to fall asleep, in the name of relaxation. This is why it's important for you to have your back unsupported and not lie down when meditating.

Technique #10: Entering Flow State

Stimulating your mind to enter the flow state is something that is an excellent exercise to carry out. Do note that you should not seek to control the state of your mind. Instead, the flow state is one of allowing, as you learned in a previous chapter when we spoke of energies. Seeking to force something is just an egotistical way of exerting control. The flow state is a channel of communication and you need to let go of your hold on the obstacles to allow it to come to you.

Setting goals that are challenging and inspiring is a great step to stimulate this. Inspiring goals that are just beyond your current comfort level in life switch your brain into creative thinking mode since you need to create a solution in order to achieve what you want. Use your conscious mind to map out a specific plan of action but don't be a stickler for it. Understand that your plans will change depending on the feedback you receive from your subconscious.

After all, you can't see the path of least resistance, so make your plans but always look for feedback from your heart. Above all else, pick simple and obvious plans to execute and resist the temptation to complicate things.

Technique #11: Yielding to Simplicity

Our conscious mind loves to complicate things since it gets an opportunity to prove how smart it is. Instead, choose the simpler option since this is likely where the path of least resistance lies and watch out for feedback. Mind you, I said simpler, not necessarily easier. The simplest option may call for hard work and spending time. In the grand scheme of things, this will cost you less than seeking alternatives, seemingly 'easier' or 'faster' options.

Yielding to simplicity may come in the form of an opportunity that will help you expand and grow. Although growth may come with stepping outside of your comfort zone, it is a necessary part of the process in order for you to manifest that which you desire. Expanding and growing as a person is yielding to simplicity, and thus allowing the universe to gift you for the person you are becoming.

Chapter 6: Do This Every Time You Take Action

Getting into a flow state requires you first to know where you wish to go. While it is easy enough to make a choice by listening to your heart, taking that first step requires another degree of awareness. Too many people seem to think that all it takes is making a choice and then life starts guiding you in the direction you need to go.

After making a choice, you need to start taking action by implementing the steps you need to take. Without this, there is no achieving your goal of choice. Doing is the most crucial step of the entire process.

Taking Action

Have you ever noticed a key quality in people who seem to keep spinning their wheels in life? These people always seem to have the qualities necessary to succeed — they have brilliant ideas and the energy to carry things out, but for one reason or another, they always remain in place, perpetually devising new ideas to move forward.

Such people often have it worse than those who fail outright because they have the illusion of success. Their ego convinces them that they're doing the right thing. They're masters of retrofitting events to justify how the world is against them, and all that takes place is coated with a veneer of positivity.

Well, the common characteristic these people share is the quality of being able to come up with brilliant ideas. They're always full of them. They have the ability to debate an idea's merits and faults to the ends of the earth and know seemingly everything about everything. Anything that you say will be met with a response that makes perfect, logical sense.

Except for the small fact that these people have no idea what it is they're talking about. They have not actually done anything and are simply talking out of theoretical knowledge and are more concerned with placating their ego's need to be seen as someone superior. Their intention is to satisfy their ego, and that's it. They end up carrying this out with due purpose.

Intention is what focuses your mind like an arrow towards its target. It is your reason for doing something. While this sounds a lot like what a goal is, in reality, intentions are like the impetus while goals are the destination. Intention is what pushes you forward, relentlessly.

As such, they are extremely powerful and make no mistake, you will carry out and do whatever your intention is. This is why it is extremely important to set it up for action and not for thinking. If you were to observe the most successful people in our world, be it in terms of financial wealth or happiness, you'll notice that their intention is completely focused on doing, not talking.

While they may spend time talking about what they do, the majority of their time is spent carrying out what they preach. Thinking about doing something ultimately costs you more energy than actually doing the thing. There are many reasons as to why people refuse to do and are content with sitting there dreaming up different ideas and to do lists.

A big reason is the ego. Your ego needs constant external validation and unfortunately, the nature of our society provides more exposure to people who talk about doing than those who actually do. The internet is full of self-proclaimed gurus who know nothing about what they're saying and only know how to manipulate their viewers' egos.

By using the promise of an idea to improve one's life, people are lured into thinking about them incessantly while providing the ego the short term boost it requires through validation of its intelligence, further driving people to seek this. Here's the thing: Thinking is easy. Doing is the tough bit. It requires you to face problems and figure out solutions.

It requires you to make yourself vulnerable and be brave by opening yourself to feedback. People who never figure out their purpose in life tend to cower behind their egos, afraid of what sort of feedback they will receive. The way past this fear is to simply define your intention.

What is your intention in life? Is it to placate your ego, or is it actually to live the best life you can? Define your intention, and you'll automatically find yourself propelled into action.

Positive Intentions in Everyday Life

At its core, setting intentions is all about recruiting energy to help propel us towards our goals. While you'd figure that your purpose alone should provide this, as we discussed before, the reality is that your purpose and goals are destinations to shoot for. In the day to day grind of things, your focus will be entirely on executing the tasks on hand to reach that goal.

Actions carried out with positive intentions have far greater power than those simply carried out for the sake of it. Intention will propel you to full awareness because this is your 'why.' When fully aware of why you're doing something, the results you produce will reflect this awareness and will move you that much closer to where you want to be.

Given their power to inform your actions, your intentions are ultimately what determines your reality. It is your intentions that determine how focused your thoughts are and how well you carry out your actions. If your intentions come from a place of positivity and in line with the nature of reality, then you will find your life turns harmonious. If it comes from a negative place, such as pleasing the ego, then you'll find your life full of unnecessary drama.

By setting your intentions in a positive manner, all sorts of hurdles disappear, and you can focus your energy much better. This is because your decision making becomes far more streamlined. For example, if you know that you intend to go west in order to achieve your goals, why would you even consider going east or north?

Without that intention to set the tone, as you begin your journey, you will need to spend time trying to figure out which direction it is you need to go. Without the framework that intention-setting provides for your thoughts, you might even go in the wrong direction for a while before realizing your mistake and then double back, which is frustrating to say the least.

Intentions help you take responsibility for your happiness and help place control right in your hands, and with this, you can live a life by design, instead of one created by habit and conditioning. It's not just in your personal life where you will see the effects of positive intentions. Look around the workplace or in any professional setting — the best leaders are those who provide their teams with a clearly defined goal.

However, beyond just setting the goal, they also make it very clear that the goal is an objective and that it must be met within certain boundaries. This is nothing but providing the team an intention to meet their day to day tasks in pursuit of that goal. This ensures everyone is pointed in the same direction and that no energy is wasted going after things that are not in line with what needs to be achieved.

Positive intention also will work wonders for your interpersonal relationships. This much is true. We tend to see the world as a reflection of ourselves. By assuming a positive viewpoint of things in your life, you'll project the same attitude onto someone else. By simply assuming positive intent from your team member, your spouse or partner, your family, and so on, you'll eliminate a lot of conflicts.

None of us are mind readers, and misinterpreting intent is one of the primary causes of conflict. We get defensive and retreat into a shell when we hear things we don't like. Well, we don't like them in the first place because we frame these things as being against our goals. By assuming that the person you're speaking to intends their comments in a positive, helpful manner, you'll be surprised at how much more open and receptive you become to feedback from life.

This has the added benefit of opening yourself up to your heart and receiving negative feedback from the infinite knowledge. Always assume positive intent from everyone you interact with, including your heart. Assume everything is set up so as to help you improve and live life with greater joy and peace. You'll find that this turns into a reality.

Set Intentions Too, Not Just Goals

Goal setting is just one half of achieving your objectives. The other half is all about setting your intentions. One of the things you must understand about intentions is that they are more of an energy than a particular statement. For example, you can define in words your intention to live your day in a particular manner.

You could wake up every day and tell yourself, "I will live today in a state of happiness and spread as much positivity to those I come in contact with."

When setting goals though, your intention is usually implicit in the goal itself. If you need to inject your career with a flush of energy, defining where you wish to be is a good starting point.

A statement such as "I am a senior xxx for company xxx" or "I own and run my business xxx which is in such and such field," will help you keep your intent focused and purposeful. These statements are goal statements but have the energy of intention within them. By reminding yourself and visualizing these as a reality, you'll inject yourself with the purpose to go out and achieve them.

By repeating such statements or statements of intentions to yourself what you're doing is activating energies within you. These energies place you in the current moment and increase your focus. Thus, a side effect of these statements is that your ego is deactivated and sidelined. When the energy level of these statements is high enough, it opens up your channel to your heart fully and gives you full access to the infinite knowledge that awaits you as you carry out your tasks.

Setting your intention is one thing, but carrying them out is another. At first, just like with meditation, your mind will wander and you will need to bring it back to the present moment and focus on your intention. This becomes easier with repeated practice, so it is a good idea to take some time every day to write down and repeat your intention statements.

Visualizing these statements as reality will charge them positively and will bring great changes into your life. Remember, your intentions have the ability to greatly influence those around you. In fact, scientific research has proven that positive human intention has the ability to influence water, which happens to be what we're mostly made up of, physically speaking.

Your intentions and the energy they transmit will interact with other people's electromagnetic fields and you will find yourself getting out of your own head more and more. Daily positive intentions have the power to get you to focus on things greater than yourself and completely minimize the ego's contribution in your life.

The more you travel outside of yourself, the more present you will be and the greater your connection to your heart will be.

Technique #12: Setting Intentions to Water

The power of intention can be used to improve your daily life through some very simple practices. The first of these practices may cause a lot of controversies, but it has its share of believers. This is the practice of setting positive intention to water. The method was conceived by Masaru Emoto, who is referred to as either a scientist or a pseudoscientist depending on which point of view you adopt.

Through experiments he conducted on setting positive intentions to water, Emoto claimed to find that the crystals of water which were formed by imparting positive emotion were of a more beautiful structure than those that were imparted with a negative energy.

Thus, he postulated that the energy transmitted through our intentions has a real impact on the molecular structure of water. Given that our bodies are almost entirely made of water, this is quite significant. There are multiple ways of transferring positive energy into the water we drink. The first is to hold a glass of water in our hands and to repeat our intention either out loud or in our minds. Our intention could be either a short term focused, daily one or something connected to our long term goals, it doesn't matter. As long as the emotion is positive and loving, you're on the right track.

A good way to further energize the water is to visualize yourself carrying out your intention and doing things in the manner you wish to. By doing this, you'll be recruiting the power of both your intention as well as visualization. Intention statements are not the only thing you can visualize and repeat.

If nothing particular strikes your mind, simply affirming a message of love and gratitude is enough to energize the water. Other things that offer you positive vibes, whether it is prayer or music, can also be used to energize the water. Consume this water intermittently throughout the day and repeat this practice before you go to bed at night.

For added effect, you could also use crystals to capture the positive energy and add this to your water prior to drinking it. In this manner, you'll build the positive energy within the water and also change the molecular structure of the water within you.

Technique #13: Setting Intentions to Statements

A far more palatable exercise for some might be the process of writing intention statements. These statements are affirmations that you can use to govern how you intend on living your life and what it is you would like to change. There are a couple of characteristics of these statements you should incorporate at all times, such as writing them in first person, using present tense.

In other words, the subject of these statements should always be you and not someone else. This would simply be you trying to control someone else's actions, and that isn't in line with the way nature works. Instead, focus on controlling your own actions and reactions to triggers.

The present tense is used to reinforce the fact that what you want in your life is real and that you have full faith that the universe will provide it for you. This is a step where quite a few people stumble. You see, you'll have faith in the realization of things that you believe possible. However, the point of setting goals and intentions is to push your limits and to achieve something that is outside your comfort zone.

Some people have confidence in themselves, but others struggle with this. For such people, writing statements they don't believe in will only reinforce their inadequacy. Thus, if you feel a negative push or have thoughts that seem to tell you that this is impossible, modify the statement.

Adding phrases such as "I am willing" or "My intention is" makes the sentence more believable and affirms to yourself that while the goal is outside your comfort zone, you're still willing to work for it and you will achieve it. This is a point of view that your brain and self-image will accept easily. So use these in place of strong statements such as "I am rich" or "I am surrounded by people who love me" and so on.

One thing to avoid is the use of words such as: try, but, and or. Your statements need to be as specific as possible. Specificity can be in the form of a quantifiable thing or in terms of emotion. What I'm saying is that you need to know if the goal or intention is met. So you can define reaching a goal in terms of feeling an emotion or in terms of something quantifiable.

A quantifiable goal is "I am a billionaire." A goal based on feeling is "I am in a loving and mutually healthy relationship." In both cases, you'll know when you get there. If you add doubt into the mix or indecision, you're scrambling your energy and conveying that this intention isn't really all that important to you and that it's okay not to follow it.

Monitor your self-talk constantly since this is just another form of stating your intention. If you detect negative talk, reframe it to positive by using the phrases mentioned previously. Always reframe negative talk and don't let it pass by without questioning and challenging it. Do this, and over time you'll find that your brain will get the message automatically correct itself.

Chapter 7: Energy of All Things

We already know that everything is connected. Nothing exists in isolation, and cause and effect is simply the proof of this fact. However, the focus of this chapter is not to dissect this phenomenon or karma or whatever you wish to call it.

Instead, we're more concerned with how things exist, in what form, and how we can better align ourselves by using this knowledge. To do this, we need to dive back into quantum physics and understand certain principles.

The Connection Between All Things

The story of quantum mechanics all begins with Neils Bohr. Bohr was the first scientist to discover that everything is made up of atoms and that surrounding these atoms, in concentric circles were electrons. These electrons vibrated at specific frequencies and thus transferred energy to the atom and the overall object. Therefore, every object had a certain energy associated with it. All this was perfectly in line with classical physics which existed since the days of Newton.

What came next was mind-boggling. Bohr expected to see the electrons behaving in the manner that classical physics would suggest. That is, much like how planets revolve around the sun, he expected to see electrons exhibiting a similar relationship to the atom they surround. Instead, he saw nothing of the sort. What he actually saw was that the electrons did not even have a physical form.

This was because the frequency at which they vibrated was so high that it was impossible to observe any physical form. Think of a rubber band that vibrates back and forth when snapped. To the naked eye, it looks as if the rubber band is in multiple places at once. This is precisely what was going on with the electrons, except at ludicrously high frequencies.

Hence, Bohr and his proteges had proved that classical physics was all wrong. That form and matter don't really exist, as Einstein commented on their findings. What we perceive as matter or form is really just a bunch of microscopic particles vibrating a low frequency so that we can perceive a form. In other words, when the rubber band stops vibrating at high speeds, we can see that it is a band. The stuff we cannot see is simply vibrating at a much higher frequency — for example, light. We know light exists thanks to it reflecting off other objects, but we can't really see light as a form.

Thus, everything in this world is just a collection of energy. After all, that's what vibration is. It is simply a representation of energy existing within something. The higher the frequency, the higher the level of energy and vibration. While the scientific community was understandably shocked by these findings, quite a few of them could not help but notice that these statements were not new. If anything, they were decidedly archaic.

They had been first uttered by the Buddha and other ancient monks whose words have been preserved over the years. These people did not have any special equipment, but the fact that they were able to deduce the same conclusions proves that energy and the universe are the same thing. Communication is not restricted to just the forms of energy on this planet, but there also exists a link between pure energy and us.

All energy is converted and transferred, and according to scientific principles, it cannot be created — although there must have been some point where all the energy in this universe was created. Call it the big bang or God or whatever, it follows that all forms of energy originate from the exact same source and thus, everything is connected to one another. There is a universal mind to which we are all connected.

The problem is that as we've gone about our lives, we've dampened this connection by wrapping ourselves in the trappings of our own worlds. We value our possessions and believe that they define us. We have forgotten that things like intention are what really matters since this is what determines our energy levels and our experience in this world.

The ego is the biggest obstacle to realizing this connection. It convinces us that these physical forms are real and these are what matter. However, this is the wrong view and this throws us off balance with the way the world really is.

Think of it this way: Have you ever met a person and immediately got a feeling about them? It could be a positive or negative one, but there's no doubt we do sense something about the people we meet.

We sometimes take an instant dislike to them or on the flip side, we instantly hit it off with them, forming lifetime friendships and more, and sometimes we even fall in love with each other at just a glance. The power of energy is undeniable.

The best public speakers often talk about feeling a room. The changes in energy within a group of people are very apparent and the ability to change energy, either increase or decrease it, is a hallmark of being able to wield influence in our world. Thus, while the law of attraction is a universal law, the reality is that there is another law that sits beneath it and governs every aspect of our existence. This is the law of vibrational frequency.

Vibrational Frequency

There is a property in physics called resonance. The way it works is this: Everything in this world has a natural frequency at which it vibrates. Vibration can be visualized as a wave that emits a certain frequency and amplitude. Amplitude here refers to the size of the waves or the energy emitted.

Thus, louder sounds are simply sound waves of a higher amplitude as are brighter lights.

When you bring another object which is vibrating at the same frequency as the natural frequency of another object, guess what happens? The second object begins to vibrate as well. This is why, when armies crossed bridges, they were told to break march since the synchronized steps produced a certain vibration that might inadvertently match the natural vibration of the bridge and cause it to twist and break apart.

When designing bridges that cross vast distances, designers have to take into account the effects of wind producing natural frequencies and inducing vibrations within the structure. Thus, the conclusion from the law of resonance is quite simple. In order to activate something in our world, you need to vibrate at its frequency. This applies equally to manifesting anything in your life.

In order to attract anything into your life, a goal or anything else, you need to vibrate at the frequency that it vibrates at. You need to match that state and resonate with it to induce it into your life. Have you ever walked into a group of people who are extremely animated and energetic? Have you been instantly energized by them?

What has happened here is that you have absorbed their energy. The old saying that you are the sum of the company you keep is very true. This simply validates the way the law of vibration works. We tend to vibrate at whatever frequency we surround ourselves with.

This is also why music resonates with us. Play your favorite music and you'll find your mood uplifted and play tracks which don't really appeal to you and you might as well draw fingernails on a chalkboard. Use this to your advantage by only focusing on music that makes you feel better and increases your vibrational state.

Aside from the people you surround yourself with, your environment also plays an important role in determining your current vibration. If you maintain an unclean and dirty environment, chances are that you will feel lazy and lethargic. Stay in a dirty locality or home and you'll start letting your own standards fall to the wayside. Vibrations induce themselves in us and it is very important to induce the correct frequencies within yourself.

Things that you see and expose yourself too also affect your frequency. If you constantly expose yourself to images of grief and struggle or images that are intended to lower your self worth (hello social media!), you will end up feeling miserable as well. Energy flows into us in a variety of ways and in the next section, I'll be giving you a couple of exercises to clear your channels. However, it all starts with filtering in the correct energy sources and choosing the right vibrations in your life.

This is precisely why gratitude is so important. Gratitude opens your eyes to how wonderful things are and puts you on a positive vibrational plane. By doing so, you will attract things that make you more grateful. Speaking positively and holding positive beliefs work in the same fashion.

Your vibrational level is also determined by the degree to which you allow the flow of energy from the universe into you. While the food you eat gets transformed into energy within you and ensures your biological functions work as planned, the free energy from the universe flows into you in the form of intuition, gut feelings, etc.

Given that this energy comes from infinite knowledge, naturally, the frequency of this energy is on a far more evolved level. Things such as stress, the ego, and giving energy to the obstacles in your life cause you to vibrate further away from this energy and you end up attracting less of it into your life.

The more universal energy you have, the more proactive you will be toward your life since you will fully assume your position as a creator and as someone who can choose the life they wish to lead. Always monitor the level of your relaxation since this is a good indicator of how much you're currently allowing universal energy within you.

By relaxation, I don't mean to say you ought to sleep all the time. What I mean is your mental and physical state. Are you constantly on edge expecting something to go wrong? Constantly worried about negativity? This only causes stress and pushes you further away from true wisdom.

Of course, all of this is just another way of saying that your thoughts ultimately matter the most. Your thoughts are just energy within you and these are what determine, more than anything else, your vibrational frequency. Thus, fix your thoughts, and you fix your life.

Thoughts Inform Your Energy

Your thoughts are instantaneous bursts of energy that travel within your brain. Think about something, and you're instantly doing it without any hesitation. Our thoughts exist on both the conscious and the subconscious plane with the latter accounting for the majority of them. By an estimate, over seventy thousand thoughts occur in the human brain throughout the day with ninety percent of that occurring in the subconscious.

There is a famous quote by Einstein, where he says that the definition of insanity is doing the same thing over and over again and expecting different results. In order to change your outer reality, you first need to change the reality that is within you. This is just a way of saying that you need to vibrate at the level of the energy you want within you, in order for it to manifest around you, through the law of resonance.

The challenge with changing your thoughts is that there is a lot of junk embedded in them — limiting beliefs, childhood conditioning, biases, judgments — all of which is just downright unhelpful. A lot of what we think is actually determined by what was installed within us when we were growing up, prior to the age of five.

At that age, our brains are not conscious, and we simply absorb whatever is around us. These thoughts are stored deep within for future use. When the time comes, some of these thoughts are discarded and the ones that remain form the basis for our actions for the rest of our lives. Unless we decide to change them, that is.

Given that your thoughts are just energy and your actions are expressions of this energy, by not giving certain energies the outlet to expend themselves, you can conceivably transform them into something else. What I mean to say is that you don't need to be a slave to every single thought that arises in your head; you have the choice to simply not act upon it. If you choose not to act on it, that energy remains within you, ready to be transformed into something else.

Transforming that latent energy is all about carrying out the actions that reflect the belief you wish to install. While thoughts inform actions, actions also inform thoughts and beliefs. Thus, if you behave in a certain manner, and visualize yourself behaving in the manner you wish to be, your brain will adopt beliefs that are in line with these actions.

In addition to visualization, we've already seen how affirmation statements can focus your intentions and get you to carry out actions that will result in massive changes in your life. A key concept to installing new beliefs that you must grasp is this: Change will not happen overnight. Those goals will not be achieved overnight. You will not live a life by design overnight. These are all built one action at a time. You need to keep repeating these new actions over and over until they get installed within you. There is no Matrix-like plug and play learning process.

There are further exercises that you can carry out, and I've listed them in the section that follows. These will help clear any blocks to universal energy you might have within you. Allowing this energy into your mind will do wonders for your understanding of what the correct beliefs are in order to live well.

You see, life is best lived when you go with the flow and don't oppose the current. You choose your stated goal and take action to progress towards it. You will meet obstacles along the way, but the universe will inform you as to which way to flow. Think of it as swimming in the ocean towards a rock which is at a distance away from shore.

When you first begin swimming, the waves will crash into you with great force, but as you go further in, you can either ride the momentum of the waves as they push you back and drag you in or you can simply swim under them. You will encounter various currents but by swimming sideways from them or with them, you navigate your way to your goal. This is how you navigate life as well in order to achieve your goals.

Technique #14: The Assemblage Point exercise

The first exercise which will enable you to allow the flow of energy within you is the Assemblage Point exercise. This exercise utilizes the power of visualization to manifest reality. It enables a full flow of universal energy within you and clears all the blocks to the universe.

To begin, stand in a relaxed manner with your feet comfortably apart. Take a few deep breaths to relax. Now, visualize a golden stream of energy entering you from below, from your feet. This energy is relaxing and moves through your body upwards. As it does so, you find that that particular portion of your body relaxes even more as you inhale. As you finish your inhalation, this golden energy exits into the universe from the top of your head.

As you begin your exhalation, visualize this golden energy now entering the top of your head and making its way down your body, through your spine and into your feet. Notice how relaxed you feel as this energy makes its way down and exits back into the universe through your feet, taking all the limiting blocks and impurities within you with it.

As you develop your ability in this exercise, you will yourself becoming more sensitive to the energy that enters you. At first, simply visualize this energy — it is more than enough to relax you and allow the energy to flow through you.

Once you have managed to relax properly with these two steps, it is now time to take things up a notch. Perform the first two steps again and after this is done, visualize both balls of energy entering you, one from the top and one from the bottom. These two pass one another as they travel through your body but they don't intersect with one another since one passes in front of your spine and the other behind it.

Try to synchronize your breath with the entry and exit of these energies from your feet and head. You can make the energy balls bigger in your imagination, but it's best to start small. The idea isn't to change the size of the energy just yet. Next, imagine that above your head is a fountain of this golden energy that is constantly pouring into you, and similarly, there is an upside-down fountain below your feet, energizing you from the bottom.

Gradually, imagine that these fountains are reaching out for one another, and eventually, they unite to form a golden sphere of pure energy around you. Feel your skin expanding with every intake of your breath as this energy continues to envelop you and protect you. Keep working on this for as long as you can.

It will be tough going at first, and you will feel tired. However, this is a muscle like everything else and the more you work at it, the better you'll be. Keep increasing the strength of the energy flowing into you gradually. Do not try to accumulate too much energy as this will throw you out of balance. Simply stick to what feels right.

Chapter 8: What it Really Takes to Manifest Wealth and Abundance

While this step is named wealth and abundance, what we're discussing in this chapter is happiness. How to figure out what it is and how to have more of it. Money and wealth are both tools as well as obstacles to this.

A lot of us have terrible beliefs about money — I simply mean imbalanced. Therefore in order to restore a sense of balance, the universe's forces do their work to balance the equation, leaving us more miserable than ever. When this happens, instead of recognizing our faulty thinking, we blame the subject of our thoughts, which in this case is money.

Abundance, wealth, money, whatever you want to call it, is simply a manifestation of what you think and how you think about it. So let's take a deeper look at this.

Money Will Not Make You Happy

Well, we might as well get the bad news out of the way first. In case it isn't apparent to you, money will not make you happy. This has never been the case and never will be. However, a lot of people take this to mean that money will never make you happy *under any circumstances*. This is false and reflects an imbalanced view of things.

Consider this scenario. It's hot outside, and you really want an ice cream to cool off. The problem is that there's no ice-cream seller or truck in sight. You're sweating profusely, and the sun is now burning a hole, seemingly, in the back of your neck as you trudge through what seems to be a hot and humid day.

You're keenly on the lookout for an ice cream vendor, and just then, you spot a truck! You run toward it and ask for your favorite flavor of ice cream and the biggest possible serving. Let's assume the size of this serving is six scoops. So as the ice cream man scoops it out one by one, into your cup, you eye it hungrily and before they can take your money, you've begun devouring the ice cream.

The first few mouthfuls are about as close to heaven as you can get. The first scoop is wonderful. The second scoop is pretty good but not as good as the first one. By the time you reach the sixth scoop, you're actively sick of ice cream because you've already had so much of it that your craving has disappeared. Whereas just a few minutes ago, you were craving ice cream and would have done anything for six scoops of ice cream, you would now gladly give away that last scoop for free.

What's going on here is known as the law of diminishing returns which affects every single one of our desires. Once we get what we want, we simply value it less. This is not to say we seek to get rid of it. Instead, it no longer occupies our minds as much. As you continue to eat the ice cream, the amount of pleasure you receive increases to a certain point, beyond which, it simply stops rising. No amount of additional ice cream can increase that.

This law applies to money as well. Beyond a certain income level, which is usually pegged at 70,000-80,000 USD per year, additional income simply doesn't give you happiness. It does give you pleasure though. This is the first obstacle you need to sort out. A lot of people mistake pleasure for happiness, but they are two completely different things.

Pleasure is the feeling of eating that first scoop of ice cream on a hot day after craving it for so long. It is mercurial and memorable. It also lasts for a very short time. It can hit high peaks but by its very nature, doesn't have a long shelf life. Happiness, on the other hand, is more like your base level of existence. It depends on some very simple things being in place, namely love and security. Shelter, food, and so on fall under the security blanket, but you could place them in separate categories as well.

Money is crucial for these things. It doesn't buy love, but you cannot exhibit your best self without the protection that money provides you with. If you're constantly worrying about how you're going to pay your next bill, always anxious about making ends meet, you're not going to attract too many potential partners to yourself. Thus, money is necessary to a certain point. It is necessary for our basic needs of security, nourishment, and of course, survival. It isn't evil or bad. It is what it is, much like what ice cream is.

How you interpret it depends on your level of balance. The more balanced you are, the truer your interpretation of things. By confusing pleasure with happiness, once people experience the comfort that money provides, and the release from the anxiety that occurs, they start chasing more money thinking that it will bring them more happiness. However, such individuals are merely chasing pleasure. Is it a surprise that these people never find happiness?

Happiness depends on some very simple things, namely, your thoughts. What is it that you think about most of the time? That is the level of your happiness. More specifically, your mindset is what determines your base level of happiness. A scarcity-based mindset, where you think everything is fleeting and that the universe takes more than it gives, will result in you creating this reality for yourself and affirming your beliefs. You will create your own truth.

Happiness depends on you adopting an abundant mindset and thus creating it for yourself. Once your basic needs are met, happiness revolves around how you choose to spend your time. In other words, what is your true purpose, and how closely aligned to it are you? Pursuing that path and realizing your progress along it is what constitutes one of the pillars of true wealth.

Much like pleasure and happiness, money and wealth have the same relationship. Money can be quantified and when you receive it after a long barren spell, it takes you to heights you will relish. However, it will never bring those same heights again once you've ascended them.

Wealth has both qualitative and quantitative aspects to it. Pleasure, happiness, and any positive emotions you experience when living your life are all indicators of wealth — these are things that cannot be quantified, but they can only be felt. Money is the quantitative aspect of wealth such as the experiences we partake in — vacations, nutrition and supplements, wellness products and fitness memberships, books and movies, events we attend, the education we seek, etc., — are all tangible aspects of having wealth. Money is what helps us attain a basic level of comfort and seek newer, expansive experiences, while the feelings we get, the results we achieve (physically, emotionally, mentally) when engaged in those experiences is what constitutes and accounts for our level of happiness and other positive emotions.

Both are necessary and complement each other. By seeing them for what they are, you will be able to adopt a balanced mindset about them. When we confuse wealth and money to be the same thing, we create major imbalances in our life which only lead to us getting rid of our money, given that we turn it into our primary source of unhappiness. Thus, we will also rid ourselves of the security provided by money and become even more miserable.

It all starts with eliminating scarcity.

How to Change Your Scarcity Mindset

Let's say you and I are eating pieces of a delicious apple pie. Both of us love the pie so we're not experiencing any diminishing returns just yet and before we know it, there's just one piece left. Now, both of us want this piece dearly and all of a sudden, it's you versus me and we've turned adversaries temporarily. All over a piece of pie.

This is exactly how people live their lives, largely speaking. They believe that the world is one large pie and there isn't enough for everyone to go around. If someone takes a larger piece, it means that the rest of us have to be content with smaller pieces. Thus, everyone is an adversary and win-win situations simply don't exist. In order for you to win, someone must lose. Pretty soon, instead of focusing on how you can win, you focus on defeating someone else. Success that is achieved in this manner, if it ever does come, is a slog and grind. There is no purpose to it and it doesn't get you out of bed in the morning.

Once that initial thrill of having bested someone subsides, there's nothing left to drive you forward and life just becomes a series of uninteresting and stressful jousts after another.

Contrast this with an abundant mindset that sees the world as it truly is. In an abundant mindset, the metaphor of the world being one large pie is a fallacy in itself. The rationale behind this is that if we are co-creators of our world and can design our life to be whatever we envision it to be, then how can there ever be a limited supply of anything? Only those who believe that resources are finite will ever believe in such nonsense. In order to live larger lives, you need to simply create it. Believing in your ability to create this is the basis of the abundant mindset.

We grow up around scarcity when we're kids. If you're like most people, you were taught that "money doesn't grow on trees," that in order to come first in your class, someone else needs to come second, and so on. While competition is a good thing and can be healthy to an extent, our school systems turn them into something they were never intended to be: a rat race where we are pitted against each other. The beauty of abundance is that by adopting this mindset, you will create more of it for yourself, since you will manifest what you focus on the most. Focus on scarcity, and you will continue living in that vicious cycle of not having enough. Focus on abundance and how you can create your own opportunities, and you will be presented with more as a result. A crucial step in cultivating an abundant mindset and manifesting your desires is recognizing your power and ability to create and manifest your desires while understanding how energy works. Simply put, you get what you focus on and direct your energy toward.

Go back and read the part about resonance if you're still unsure about how this works and why this is true. Next, commit to improving yourself in small steps every single day. It doesn't matter how small the step is, simply take one to improve yourself and commit to it, every single day. Improving yourself can mean learning a new skill or reinforcing an old one. Keep your mind fresh by giving it a workout and providing it with novelty.

Novelty is a highly underrated tool when it comes to mental development. Exposing your mind to new things will help it navigate change better and will also expand your world considerably. By doing this, you're squarely attacking the idea that the world is a limited place. After all, if there are so many things in the world to learn, how can it ever be limited? Thus, explore ideas and concepts every day that expand your understanding of the world. This is what true self-development is.

Next, study and learn from others' mistakes and successes. The whole world is at your disposal and it functions as a sounding board for your ideas. If you wish to do something, explore whether others have done it and see how it worked out for them. Once our ancestors discovered fire and invented the wheel, there was no need for us to do the same every single time. We simply applied and refined their processes.

Similarly, there have been generations of brilliant women and men who have come before you who have experienced life in much the same manner as you. Seek to learn from them and absorb their learning from the mistakes they made. This way, you can dramatically improve your life since you will be tapping into a higher level of consciousness than just your own when it comes to learning.

One of the mistakes people make is when they realize how truly wonderful the abundant mindset is, they become hard on themselves and admonish themselves for having adopted a scarcity mindset for so long. Don't be too hard on yourself. After all, you're just as entitled to make mistakes as the next person. Learn from this and move on.

Being mindful of your thoughts and actions is a great practice for you to carry out. Practicing mindfulness will keep you rooted in the present, which will help you realize just how abundant the world is. Think about the present moment for a second. It is always there and it has no end. Anything can happen within this.

The past, in contrast, as well as the future is always fixed. It doesn't flow but it ends at a certain point once your projection and imagination runs out. Thus, it is limited. There is no sense of possibility with them since you can only come up with so many scenarios. However, the present moment depends on forces much larger than you and I. The possibilities are endless. If this is not abundance, what is?

Lastly, the most powerful way to develop an abundant mindset is to practice gratitude and altruism, or giving. More than anything else, these two things will guarantee an abundant mindset and true happiness, because of the simple principle: What you give is what you will receive. Let's take a look at this fantastic phenomenon.

Generosity

Buddhist practice always emphasizes the importance of giving. Look around society and you'll often find that the happiest people are those who give back to the community. There is however, a danger of giving for the wrong reasons. Too many people look at charity as a means of inflating their egos and don't give with the right intentions.

The act of giving opens up your mind to abundance more than anything else because it teaches you that you can literally afford to give things away. In other words, you are prosperous. No matter what problems you think you're dealing with, you can still afford to improve someone else's life.

According to Buddhist thought, the act of giving is far more powerful when it is carried out in favor of someone who is worthy as opposed to someone who doesn't deserve it. Now, this could be misinterpreted to mean that the poorest in society do not deserve charity, which is certainly not the case.

The truth is that determining who deserves charity and who doesn't is a purely personal choice and the motive behind charity should be to feel gratitude and thankfulness — for what you have and how grateful you feel to be able to be a blessing to others and help them better their lives. Your aim should not be something material in this regard.

Gratitude is an important practice for you to follow and quite simply, it is the most positive state of mind you can adopt. By being thankful for your blessings and looking at what you have, as opposed to what you don't have yet, you are further reinforcing the abundance of this world.

The fact of the matter is that human civilization is currently at its peak. In the west, we've never lived longer, had more comfortable lives or technology to aid us. However, we're more miserable than ever. This is solely due to a lack of focus on gratitude. We have it better than large parts of the world, but all we ever focus on is the lack of things or settling political scores.

Ultimately, it all boils down to what you want in your life. Put out positive energy and gratitude, you will receive it back tenfold thanks to the principle of resonance. Always take the time to relax and count your blessings. By blessings, I mean focusing on the positive things in your life despite the multitude of things that may not always be on point.

You'll find that all your problems will soon have solutions and that your life will move forward positively. Give whatever you can, without any need for reciprocation or don't give at all. Focus on feeling good when you give and make this your objective. Remember to differentiate between the fleeting feeling of pleasure and true happiness when you set your objective to give.

The practices for this chapter have already been talked about and explained, but I will sum it up for you here. Simply focus on being grateful for what you have and give more of what you want to develop abundance. With these simple practices you can reprogram your mind to believe that you already have what you want. With this, comes a paradigm shift that changes your external reality to correlate with your internal reality. Stop thinking of what you don't have and begin thinking of all the possibilities that exist for something wonderful to happen in your life.

Chapter 9: How to Create Your Best Life

One of the most powerful techniques you can use to improve your life is to utilize the power of imagination. Too often, those who have powerful imaginations get castigated as daydreamers or as those who aren't realistic. Well, imagination is the key to creation because if you can't see it in your head, you're unlikely to see it in real life.

Think of how popular movie directors go about their work or how artists approach their craft. They first begin by visualizing exactly how whatever it is they wish to produce will look like and how it will feel. Much like a movie or a beautiful picture, you too have the ability to direct your life in this manner.

In this chapter, we will show you exactly how you can do this.

The Power of Imagination

Do you know that your brain has no way to tell what is real and what is imagined? As far as it is concerned, if the visualized picture feels real enough, it adopts it as if it really happened. You see, consciousness and reality can be manipulated by strong visuals and emotions. Think back to some old memories of yours and you will find that while you feel things happened one way, the reality is that things were slightly different.

We tend to believe that whatever we get to experience is reality. However, with enough sensory information about an event added to our mental picture, we will end up experiencing the imagined picture as real as well.

In a nutshell, *this* is the power of visualization. Your ability to build pictures, which you know are not real but are nonetheless being created with the intention to improve your life is a direct testimony to your ability to be a creator.

Never underestimate the power of your imagination to create worlds for you. Using this tool, you get to experience an entire universe of possibilities, therefore truly freeing yourself since there is nothing and nobody else constraining you, but yourself, inside your head. One of the key indicators of a powerful mental image is its ability to transport you using your other senses.

We all have moments in our lives that have impacted us and shaped us profoundly. These moments create particular imprints on our senses — visual, sensory (taste, smell, sound, touch) or a feeling of some kind. This is one way to imagine and visualize your desired life. Thus far, you're probably just using your ability to imagine as idle daydreaming.

Visualizing pictures without consciously working to attain them is daydreaming. However, once you begin infusing them with the power of your intentions and goals, and practice visualization with discipline and faith, you will see these pictures manifest themselves in the real world. Will they be exactly as what you visualized? Maybe or maybe not. However, there's no denying that the essence of your visualization will come true in your life.

Imagination is integral to the entire process, and it is crucial that you let it roam freely. Use your imagination in a positive manner and watch how your life changes. Most of us are actually experts at imagination, but we simply don't realize it. Think back to when you felt anxious or sad about anything.

Your mind was producing pictures and imagining outcomes that hadn't yet occurred, which resulted in causing you to feel anxious and sad. Thus, instead of using the power of imagination to feel bad, simply turn this around and use it to feel good instead. Construct a life that you want and fill it with images and feelings that you desire.

Imagination also taps into the powerful placebo effect of healing. Simply put, our minds are easily influenced by whatever reality is imposed upon them. Numerous studies have shown that a powerful imagination can speed up recovery after an accident or illness. Imagine both the bird's and the worm's eye view of details in your visualization. This way, you'll fill in the details on all levels and will actively engage with your vision, thereby directing more of your focus towards it.

One of the best ways to utilize your imagination powerfully is by pairing it with a meditation technique.

Meditation with Visualization

The benefits of meditation have already been touched upon previously. There are a number of techniques you can use in your meditation practice

— pairing meditation with visualization is just one of them. As a matter of fact, there are different ways in which you can use visualization to increase the potency of your meditation practice.

The first technique is to meditate with a focus on liberating the mind from every day worries. All you need to do is practice meditating using your usual technique every day in a disciplined manner. After a period of time, you will find that you will have access to your inner mind and its thoughts.

This inner mind is nothing but the subconscious mind, which is a sum of all of your beliefs as well as knowledge from the heart. When you first gain access to this inner layer, you will start seeing images and visuals in your head, which will guide you in a certain direction in your life. These images can be used as pointers for your next course of action.

Using meditation to clear your mind before your visualization practice is typically a great idea. This way, your mind will be calmer and more focused on the images you wish to create. The way to do this is by meditating as usual but ending your meditation with a visualization. Before meditation, pick a general topic you wish to visualize and create in your life. Fill it with an appropriate level of detail, as you feel. There's no right or wrong level of detail.

Once you've finished meditating, visualize the images in your mind and add as many details as you wish. Focus on making these pictures as real as possible by adding sensory information to these pictures and emotional impact as well. If you're not able to come up with visual imagery, simply use visualization to heal yourself.

Visualize yourself in nature, either a forest or on a hilltop or any natural surroundings which you prefer. Interact with this environment in your mind and note all the sensory information. This way, you will calm yourself and place yourself in a good spot in order to spread the gift of your love.

Your heart is the center of love and joy in your body — visualize it as beaming with golden energy, which is pure love. Imagine this power coursing through your body and then visualize sending this energy to your loved ones or to a destination of your choice via your palms. You can use your imagination to alter the future outcomes of past actions as well.

Once you've finished meditating, run the pictures of the past event in your mind once again. Remember to use as much information as possible and add as much sensory data as possible. Think about what you felt, what sort of touch you experienced, what emotions you felt as the event unfolded, what did other people or things in the picture experience, and so on. Detail is the key to making things as realistic and lifelike as possible.

Now, as you run the pictures in your mind, alter the elements you wish to change. For example, perhaps you reacted in a negative manner to something so now visualize yourself as reacting in the manner you wish you had reacted. Again, feel this new picture as deeply as possible in order to install it completely into your brain.

At first, your brain will likely reject this new picture, but continue doing this and over time you will find that your memory of this event changes completely. Build your pictures in layers and don't be in a rush to fill out your scenes all at once. So don't expect to have fully formed visions in your head after just one session of doing this.

Most of us are accustomed to using this power in a sparing and unconscious manner so it will take time to do so consciously. Fill in the main details and then add some atmosphere or color to the scenery. Next, infuse emotion and finally add the tiny details such as particular actions or the sensory information of certain inanimate elements in the picture.

Meditation will make the entire process easier since you will have a greater ability to focus your mind's energies and create exactly what you want.

Multi Sensory Visualization

The process of using your senses to make your mental pictures more real might be confusing at first, so it's worth to go into this in a bit more detail. While most people are visually dominant, for some, the other senses might be more impactful. Then, there are certain scenarios that provoke an equal sensory response, other than just that of sight.

For example, if I ask you to visualize a beach, the first thing you probably hear is the sound of waves. Similarly, if I were to ask you to visualize a waterfall, it is the sound of the waterfall, which will likely come to mind at first thought. When visualizing rainfall, it is the touch of the water on your skin or the smell of the earth when the rain first hits that come to your mind.

As you visualize, play around with the various senses you can detect. Paint the original picture visually if necessary, but don't restrict yourself to just the visual image. Sticking with the beach example, your first step might be to paint a picture visually. Imagine the sun on the horizon casting an orange glow over everything as the waves crash onto the sparkling white sand.

You might choose to add people to this scene or leave the beach empty. How about the palm trees lining the beach? Add some hammocks or other accessories as you please. As you're doing this, become aware of the sounds that the waves make. Keep this in your awareness as you visualize this scene.

Next, add the sounds of the birds on the shoreline to your awareness. See them visually and add their chirping to the soundtrack, along with the sounds of the ocean. As you walk along the sand, notice how the sun feels on your skin. Does it feel searingly hot or pleasant and comfortable? Experience how this feels and assimilate this into your overall picture.

Next, become aware of how the sand feels between your toes. The sand probably feels dry and irritating. There might be some stones in there as well. As you get closer to the water, the sand firms up and the feeling of wetness can be detected by your toes. Furthermore, you're closer to the waves now, so the sound of the ocean is much louder and drowns out everything else.

Can you hear the sound of the spray as it washes ashore? It sounds like a hiss as the water recedes back into the ocean. Whether you choose to enter the water or remain ashore and walk along the water's edge, continue adding more sensory input into the picture.

As your ability to handle sensory input grows, start adding other living things into the picture such as other people or animals, and so on. Imagine their behaviors and reactions as your senses record them. Whatever it is you choose to add, remember to focus on how good the picture feels and the swell of positive emotion that is growing within you. This positive emotion should underline everything in your scene at all times.

To some, everything I've just written will seem like common sense, but for those who really struggle with visualization and can't seem to build any power into their pictures, this example will help flesh out a lot of things. In such cases, I recommend starting small with an equally small intention. Simply visualize walking on the beach and feeling good. That's it.

Don't add anything extra like the sound of the waves or the specifics of your location. Simply feel the sand, hear the sea, and look a few steps ahead as you feel good. Building your picture slowly will get your brain accustomed, and soon, you will be building complex pictures using your mind and even better, having these manifest into reality.

Technique #15: Meditation and Visualization with Emotion

As mentioned before, meditation is a practice that will take your visualization practice to the next level, thanks to its ability to help you minimize mental distractions. There are many meditation practices you can choose to follow. The most common starting point for most people is simply becoming aware of their breath.

While that exercise increases your overall awareness, you can develop your focus by tweaking it a little bit. Start off by relaxing your body and becoming aware of your breath. Once your mind quiets down a bit, count your breaths up to twenty. When reaching twenty, count backwards to one.

The trick is, as you're counting, if you find yourself getting distracted by other thoughts or images that pop into your mind, you need to reset the count. The first time you do this, you'll struggle to get past three, so remember that getting a high count isn't all that important.

What is important is that you simply notice how unfocused your mind can be. Keep persisting and resetting the count. If you manage to get a high number and you've never meditated before, you're probably not aware enough of your mind to begin with so I suggest going back to the breathing exercise to build it up first. Any picture that flashes in your mind's eye or any thought that pops up counts as a distraction where you need to reset the count.

Remain patient with this exercise and don't do this for more than five minutes in the beginning. You will find yourself becoming tired when doing this in the beginning, but keep persisting with it and you'll find that your ability to focus your mind increases exponentially.

The other exercise you can do is simply setting aside some time every day to visualize your future. This is the future that you choose and deeply want and are willing to work toward making it happen. Remember, just like your intention, this picture needs to be measurable in some form so you can identify and know when you're there. This could either be in some material way or as an emotion.

Beware of the dangers of chasing pleasure if you decide to define your goal in terms of material terms. It is far better to set an emotion to your picture and then, just as in the example in the previous section, begin building your picture step by step. The truly powerful visualizations are one where the heart and the brain come together.

Thus, aligning your visualized pictures to your purpose, your intention, and your goals is what will bring it into reality. This is the best way of signaling your intent to the universe and getting yourself vibrating at a more positive frequency in order to attract what it is you desire.

Always feel the positive emotion from the scene since this is what causes you to vibrate on a better plane. The emotion you feel is the most important and when it becomes deep enough and the pictures are real enough, you'll actually see them with your eyes open, either when they manifest around you or when you go about your daily tasks, you'll be able to access that feeling without any problems.

Chapter 10: Becoming Fully Alive

What is the nature of this universe we live in? How do we surrender to its current yet chart our own course? This book thus far has dealt with these questions in detail and now, it is time to take things one step further. You see, to fully commit yourself to the way things ought to be and to extract everything that life has to offer, we need to delve into a few more fundamentals.

Things such as belief and faith, feedback loops from the universe, the power of patience, and lastly dispelling your fear of yourself will be discussed in this chapter.

Faith and Belief

Anyone who has ever undertaken a trip to the other side of the world, usually places like Indonesia, Thailand, India, etc., has encountered all forms of spiritual awareness. Some of these actually work and are not some elaborate hoax. Spirituality has a religious angle to it, and indeed, every religion seems to start off as a bunch of spiritual beliefs which then get warped into something else entirely, and call for faith.

The call for faith is an interesting phenomenon since in reality, what a lot of religions and people who cling onto dogma demand is belief, not faith. Beliefs are statements that are held as truth and are not allowed to be questioned. Think of how strongly you hold onto your own beliefs about the world and feel uncomfortable every time they are challenged or questioned.

Belief requires you to adopt a narrow mindset of things and stick to a narrow path — a path that hinders growth and expansion. Anything outside this path is simply deemed irrational and wrong. Ironically, a person who believes the most claims to have the highest degree of faith. This is categorically untrue. Faith is the exact opposite of belief. Faith requires you to open your mind and consider a variety of options and to be comfortable with ambiguity, with not knowing which one is right.

While belief demands that you hold onto something — an outcome, a fundamental system, an answer — and never let go, faith demands no such thing. Instead, faith merely asks that you keep an open mind and evaluate things based on your understanding of the truth — an objective truth. An analysis of any religious text will result in this sort of philosophy. However, this doesn't serve the needs of narrow-minded spiritual leaders, and hence, belief and faith are often switched around. Faith is needed at the start of any spiritual practice but should never morph into belief.

This would simply be adopting a position of imbalance in the universe, which, to your own detriment, would soon be corrected and brought to equilibrium thanks to the natural forces of energetic balance. The conflict between science and religion often reflects the misunderstanding that occurs when you have two sides clinging to their own beliefs. No one really wins in such cases since beliefs are self-affirming and are immune to attack, unless the individual who holds these beliefs wishes to change them.

Given that these people have adopted an extremist view, it is unlikely they wish for change, and thus the cycle continues. The truth is that everything is one, and everything exists in one large feedback loop. To say that science is against spirituality is to argue that your leg is against your arm.

The rate of change that is currently occurring in our society on a global level requires us to adopt an attitude of faith. Faith is the willingness to accept whatever comes, no matter what the truth will be. Faith is believing in an abundant universe and in the justification for everything to exist. This is what enables us to live life to the fullest and interact with our environments successfully.

Both our environment and us exist in a feedback loop that impacts us on a daily basis. Given the rate at which our environments are changing, it is natural that we should feel a sense of imbalance, which is only made worse by trying to cling onto beliefs. Let us examine this feedback loop a bit more.

Ontological Designers

Ontological design is a fancy way of saying that the way our world is designed affects us and that we, in turn, affect the way our world is designed. It goes beyond saying that our environments affect us or that our socio-cultural values, beliefs, and norms affect us. Ontological design takes into account that the feedback loop exists, whereas these latter statements don't.

Taking the example of language, we are born into a particular language and use it to think and to express ourselves. Our ability to enunciate our thoughts depends directly on the language and our beliefs are formed by it as well. In turn, we also modify the language and thus reinforce the feedback loop. A good example of this is how new words come into being to describe phenomena that have sprung into the environment recently.

Prime examples of this are "fake news" and "alternative facts." Both these phrases warp the original meaning of the terms they describe but do a very good job of describing the current information cycle. There are simply too many sources of news to monitor, and there's no way of knowing immediately which one is right and which one is wrong.

Thus, every single fact has now been opened up for questioning, and by doing this, there is a growing movement of irrationality. The flat earth movement is such an example. By simply covering the existence of such people, the movement gains more followers.

Please note that I'm toning down a lot of the heavy philosophy on this topic. If you're interested in this, you can refer to the academic paper written by Anne-Marie Willis. The really interesting bit is to figure out what all of this means. Well, in short, it means that the process of effecting change has transformed.

While change previously was a bottom-up phenomenon, perhaps moving forward, the best way to induce change is to start from within. This form of change starts with a trigger from our environment. In turn, the change, when it manifests, affects our environment and thus the feedback loop perpetuates.

This has significant implications for the design of technology, which has transformed human behavior to an extent never seen before. However, from a more personal standpoint, it means that to manifest a change in your future, you need to interact with your environment and start things in motion. Once this motion begins, your environment will act back upon you, and thus, you will end up realizing your vision.

This is in contrast to the typical advice about manifesting, which proposes that visualization and positivity are all you need and that the universe will bring it to you. Nothing is farther from the truth. You need to go out and engage with your environment and gain feedback in order to move forward.

Thus, when designing your vision for the future, don't start with what sort of an environment you want. Instead, begin with what sort of a person you wish to be and work from there. What sort of qualities do you wish to develop in yourself? How do you wish to interact with the world? By designing your future self, you will end up designing your environment.

In turn, this environment will give you feedback, and as both of you interact with one another, both change and thus, your future self and vision are realized. How soon will this future be realized? Well, the universe works in its own ways and remember, time is not real. We tend to measure everything by clock time and make the mistake of thinking of everything in these terms.

To fully manifest your visions, it is essential for you to adopt faith and to accept whatever comes, while still taking action from an intentional, purposeful place. The key quality to all of this is thus, patience.

Patience

The hardest part of anything is the wait. Time once again plays tricks on us and reminds us of how it isn't real when we're forced to wait for something we want desperately. When you were a kid, waiting to unwrap your presents for the following Christmas morning was intolerable. You couldn't wait for night to be over and wake up the next morning to open up your gifts from under the tree. Odds are, this was the only day you managed to wake up early as well.

The same pattern plays out when you make your choice and then wait for it to manifest. You focus on your intention and carry out the tasks that will take you toward your goals. Then a month goes by. Then another. And nothing changes. You're still in the same place, dealing with the same things and putting up with the same crap that you wish to get away from in the first place.

So what's going on here? Well, first off, when making a choice, a lot of people stumble and choose things they wish to avoid. In other words, instead of wishing to become wealthy, for example, they wish to be "not poor." Choices don't work like that. You see, by choosing the opposite of something, while your language implies a desire to move away from it, your attention is doing the exact opposite.

Think of it this way. When running away from say, a bear in the wilderness, your attention is focused on the bear despite the fact that you're running away from it. This is out of necessity since you need to know where it is and how close it is to you, especially if it's chasing you. However, in situations that are not life-threatening and when dealing with metaphysical realities, focusing your attention on what you don't want doesn't save you from it. It only puts you in a pattern of constantly avoiding it, narrowly.

This is why you should focus on the positive aspect of anything rather than the negative. Avoiding some discomfort is still focusing on the discomfort, and instead of directing that energy toward your solution, you are paying more energy to your obstacle and hence encountering more of that. To illustrate the correct approach, let's use the example of a race car driver.

A fundamental instruction that competitive racers receive is that when the vehicle slides out of control, instead of looking at where the vehicle is headed, look to where you want the vehicle to go instead. Thus, when a car loses grip in a corner and begins to slide towards the wall, you'll always see the driver looking at the corner and not the barrier.

Similarly, when taking a corner, you'll notice that racers never look at the corner but always a few feet ahead of it, at the path they wish to guide their vehicle along. Use the same principle in your life. Always look at where you want to go instead of what you wish to avoid.

If you're doing this properly and you find that the thing you desire still isn't manifesting, then you simply need to wait. Remember that you do not have the full body of knowledge in your sights. You don't know what the universe has planned for you along the path you have chosen, and it is simply a matter of time before you find out.

Your choice is like planting a seed in the soil. Digging up the seed after a week or a month because it is doing nothing, despite you watering and caring for it, is the height of irrationality. Yet, we do this so often in our own lives.

Make your choice and nurture it consistently by maintaining discipline and visualizing your goals. Carry out all your tasks with the right intention, and you'll find that you'll manifest your vision before you know it. The key is to maintain your attention on the journey and not on the goal for the most part. Remain in journey mode and focus on where you wish to go within the next few steps.

This way, you'll cultivate patience automatically and live a purposeful life.

The Jonah Complex

The story of Jonah from the Bible is one of running away from one's true destiny and the repercussions of that. Now, I'm not pushing a religious angle here, just that it's a great story with a good nugget of wisdom. In case you aren't familiar with it, this is how it goes. God delivers a message to Jonah, a prophet. The message is that Jonah needs to travel to the city of Nineveh and deliver a prophecy of doom should its inhabitants continue along their current path of excess.

Jonah, who abhors Nineveh and considers its doom predestined, resists providing Nineveh's citizens this warning because he wishes to guarantee what he thinks ought to happen. He sails away on a ship to avoid his task, but soon a storm strikes and Jonah is thrown overboard, willingly by his shipmates. He's swallowed by a whale and is transported to dry land where he delivers his prophecy. Much to his surprise, the Ninevites repent and escape destruction.

There are a lot of lessons here but for the purposes of our discussion, let's focus on the ignorance of divine calling and its futility. No matter how much Jonah resists, he is pulled back toward his purpose, and when he does carry it out, he finds greater wisdom than he originally supposed.

Your purpose and you have a similar relationship. A lot of us are afraid or unwilling to carry it out and journey toward it thanks to presupposed ideas often held by those around us. Abraham Maslow observed this effect and mentioned in his works that human beings are often afraid of their own potential. How many of you reading this have it in you to compose the most beautiful musical symphonies? How many of you can change the world and eradicate poverty from it?

Answering 'yes' to those questions in the moment is one thing. Constantly believing in it is another. Doubts will creep up, the inner voice will ask "Who, you?" in response to your goals and slowly, but surely, we'll downsize our goals to something more palatable and believable. We'll begin seeking security and comfort which stems from conformity and satisfy ourselves with attaining exactly what everyone else around us wants — what they think is possible for us, what they believe is possible for us — what they themselves desire.

There's nothing wrong in wanting what everyone else desires. Things such as money, comfort, a soul mate, children, and so on. However, these are things that the universe provides to you as long as you set your intentions toward them. Your purpose is usually a very different beast. It scares you because of how grand it is and when you glimpse it, even if for a brief moment, you stand in awe of how inspiring and motivating it is.

That same awe also works in the other direction, pushing you down once the initial feeling subsides because none of us see ourselves as anything close to perfect. We often compare our flaws to other people's perfections. Hence, when we even dare to get a glimpse of the perfect nature of our purpose, we can't help but highlight our flaws. How can someone who barely understands music rival Beethoven, who managed to compose ethereally beautiful and life-changing musical symphonies despite being deaf?

Opening yourself up to your purpose is simply bringing yourself closer to divine energy — an energy we cannot comprehend. You have been placed in the scheme of things with a mission. A mission in which you distribute your gift to the world. Your gift is simply the realization of your purpose. Thus, you owe it to yourself and to the world to pursue it.

So, stop running away from what you were meant to do and who you were meant to be. Go ahead and engage with life to the fullest. Ironically, this is when you'll be the most alive and in greatest touch with who you truly are.

Conclusion

How does one live their best life? This has been the underlying topic throughout this book. We began by exploring the true nature of reality and ended by examining how to truly live life at its fullest. The energy that courses through you is the same as what courses through everything else in this world. You are a part of everything as much as everything is a part of you.

Your life is really just a series of choices, and every possible choice is available to you, right now, in this very moment. Much like a tree with infinite branches, you choose your way to the purpose that is important to you. Once your choice is made, sit back and get into journey mode. By journey mode, I mean to say that your focus should be on the everyday tasks and goals you need to implement and achieve in order to bring your journey into fruition.

Along the way, you will encounter obstacles and this is necessary. Everything has a justification for existing and the knowledge that brought the obstacle into reality isn't fully available to us, and neither is it necessary. What is required, however, is a focus on our path and where we wish to go. The universe works through balance, and the forces within it will make sure to restore balance wherever there is excess energy being stored or generated.

These forces will usually result in negative consequences for you, so maintaining balance is paramount. Using the power of intentions and goal setting, you can remain on your path and maintain focus on your journey. While it is good to visualize yourself as arriving at your chosen destination, constantly living in the future is like missing the beauty of the entire forest. Much like a train journey through beautiful scenery, if you focus on merely arriving at your destination, you'll miss out on a lot in between. Stop caring so much about your destination and instead know that you will arrive when you need to. Meanwhile, focus on the path you're taking and listen to the universe as it speaks to you.

You may speak with words, but remember, the universe speaks through emotion and intuition. Your heart is your connection to the universe and its wisdom. It has access to infinite intelligence and knows what is best for you. Often, the messages of fear and intuition are confusing. Remember that time does not exist and that fear needs time in order to function.

Examine your feelings, and if you find that they have a dimension of time attached to them, then this is merely your ego driving things. Your ego requires time, and the contrast it provides is so it can function and thrive. Emotional drama, usually negativity, is what nourishes the ego. Press the brakes on it by simply focusing on the present, the now, which is the only moment anyone really has.

The current moment is boundless and exists forever. You need not worry about it coming to an end and can simply focus on what it is you need to do. Intuition lives in the present moment and is accompanied by a feeling of comfort, even if it doesn't always make sense. Listen to it and trust its voice.

Once you achieve synchronicity between your heart and mind, it is time to get out of your own way. Detach yourself from your goals and develop the attitude of faith in everything. Remember to differentiate between the attitudes of faith and belief. Belief is rigid and is simply a product of the ego. Belief requires you to reject faith only asks that you accept if possible.

Faith is an open state of mind and asks for acceptance of things that are beyond our control. Maintaining a state of faith, as opposed to belief, is what will put you in line with the way the universe works. Yield to the path of least resistance which will make itself available to you, thanks to your connection with the infinite. Follow the lead of your intuition and heart.

The relationship between universal laws and quantum physics is well established. Reality exists on a plane that we cannot fully comprehend and it is faith that sustains us as we move along the path of truth. Everything in our universe has an energetic vibration, and in order to achieve resonance with anything, we need to vibrate at its frequency. Thus, in order to change your life, changing your thoughts —which are just vibrations — is essential.

Thought patterns are vibrations we put out into the universe, and the energy we dispel is what we receive in return. Similar to the classical third law of motion in Newtonian physics, every action has an equal and opposite reaction. The effects of this law can be seen in the quantum field as well and in our lives. Striving to live life to the fullest is the only true way to live, embracing the awe it produces within us.

Designing our lives is a matter of changing what is within us and manifesting it in our outer environment. Changing our environment produces an equal change within us, and this relationship exists as a feedback loop. Thus, respecting our environment and engineering it to be as supportive of our cause is crucial. Respect what is around you, and you will find yourself becoming better and bettering it in return. This is the reality of all things and the interconnectedness that exists everywhere.

The purpose of life is to pursue wealth — the wealth of mind, body, spirit, and of course, material wealth. Wealth is a very different thing from money, and understanding the differences is crucial. Remember that nothing, including money, is bad. As chemists often say, it is the dosage that is the difference between medicine and poison. Money provides comfort, but do not mistake it to be a source of happiness. Wealth brings happiness, while excess money brings pleasure. Both are a part of one another and are as necessary as one another. Maintain a balance between this relationship and see your life blossom.

Lastly, remember that you are the supreme creation of the infinite. You are the most evolved and creative of all species of life on this planet. Stop running away from who you are meant to be and live life to the fullest. Engage with that which speaks to you and listen to your heart and trust it infinitely.

References

Almeida, F. (2019). Being and Design: Anne-Marie Willis on the hermeneutics of our creations. Retrieved 30 July 2019, from https://www.pantagruelista.com/blogeng/being-and-design

Cho, W. (2017). The Jonah Complex — Fear of your own greatness. Retrieved 30 July 2019, from https://mystudentvoices.com/the-jonah-complex-fear-of-your-own-greatness-47d9e8d41ab5?gi=a514f580acce

Energetic Communication. (2019). Retrieved 6 August 2019, from https://www.heartmath.org/research/science-of-the-heart/energetic-communication/

Fraser, J. (2017). How The Human Body Creates Electromagnetic Fields. Retrieved 30 July 2019, from https://www.forbes.com/sites/quora/2017/11/03/how-the-human-body-creates-electromagnetic-fields/#72add80256ea

How Beliefs Are Formed and How to Change Them. (2019). Retrieved 30 July 2019, from http://www.skilledatlife.com/how-beliefs-are-formed-and-how-to-change-them/

Loeffler, J. (2018). Niels Bohr's Quantum Mechanics and Philosophy of Physics. Retrieved 30 July 2019, from https://interestingengineering.com/niels-bohrs-quantum-mechanics-and-philosophy-of-physics

Medrut, F. (2017). 25 Henry Ford Quotes to Make You Feel Like You Can Achieve Anything | Goalcast. Retrieved 30 July 2019, from https://www.goalcast.com/2017/12/24/henry-ford-quotes/

Munnangi S, Angus LD. Placebo Effect. [Updated 2019 Mar 23]. In: StatPearls [Internet]. Treasure Island (FL): StatPearls Publishing; 2019 Jan-. Available from: https://www.ncbi.nlm.nih.gov/books/NBK513296/

Oppong, T. (2018). Ikigai: The Japanese Secret to a Long and Happy Life Might Just Help You Live a More Fulfilling Life. Retrieved 30 July 2019, from https://medium.com/thrive-global/ikigai-the-japanese-secret-to-a-long-and-happy-life-might-just-help-you-live-a-more-fulfilling-9871d01992b7

Sarah Knapton. (2017). Mothers and babies brain waves synchronize when they gaze at each other, scientists find. Retrieved 30 July 2019, from https://www.telegraph.co.uk/science/2017/11/29/mothers-babies-brainwaves-snychronise-gaze-scientists-find/

Sasson, R. (2019). How Many Thoughts Does Your Mind Think in One Hour?. Retrieved 7 August 2019, from https://www.successconsciousness.com/blog/inner-peace/how-many-thoughts-does-your-mind-think-in-one-hour/

Science of Water. (2019). Retrieved 30 July 2019, from https://www.masaru-emoto.net/en/science-of-messages-from-water/

The Information Interpretation of Quantum Mechanics. (2016). Retrieved 30 July 2019, from http://www.informationphilosopher.com/introduction/physics/interpretation/

Thum, M. (2008). Clock Time vs. Psychological Time. Retrieved 30 July 2019, from https://www.myrkothum.com/the-difference-of-clock-time-and-psychological-time/

www.ingramcontent.com/pod-product-compliance
Lightning Source LLC
Chambersburg PA
CBHW060357080526
44583CB00012B/357